The Presidency Is Not A Joke

The Presidency Is Not A Joke

Observations of the character of George
W. Bush's Presidency
(From the diary of a voter)

Ernest A. Ndukwe, Ph.D.

Writers Club Press
San Jose New York Lincoln Shanghai

The Presidency Is Not A Joke
Observations of the character of George W. Bush's Presidency
(From the diary of a voter)

Writers Club Press
an imprint of iUniverse, Inc.

For information address:
iUniverse, Inc.
5220 S. 16th St., Suite 200
Lincoln, NE 68512
www.iuniverse.com

Could be located in other sections including civics, public policy etc

ISBN: 0-595-22114-9

Printed in the United States of America

To my wife Obianuju, my children Chioma, Chinenye and Amauche and to my parents Mrs.Augusta and late Mr. Silas Ndukwe.

Contents

Introduction

The title of this book came to my mind during the 2000 presidential campaign between the then Governor George W. Bush and the then former vice president Al Gore. I saw two candidates. One was very experienced in national and international politics. The other has been the governor of Texas for about five years but with limited national and international political experience. In my opinion, the press (most in print and television) handled the campaigns like it was a joke. Lots of time were spent on Bush's gaffes and jokes but the presidency is not a joke. It does not take great imagination to reason that the American president has one of the toughest jobs in the world. Some will argue it is the toughest job in the world but in my thinking, being an American president has to be a little easier than presiding over a country that is lawless, riddled with corruption, mismanagement, coups and counter coups with military dictatorship, lack of free press and lack of a reasonable constitution. Just ruling by decrees with some elements of enraging civil wars. A few countries around the world fit my hypothetical example. Those who govern them must have very tough jobs too.

One of the dangers of people such as politicians espousing their 'good' character is that they invite a closer examination or scrutiny from others. In the 2000 presidential campaign, I watched with interest as one candidate and his supporters talked and demolished the other with the character issue. Al Gore was called a liar and it stuck. George W. Bush (affectionately referred to as "Dubya" according to Molly Irvins, the humorous columnist from Texas, was the governor of Texas. He presented himself as one from 'outside Washington, D.C.' and as the good guy, one you can trust, the

honest and truthful one. His supporters bought that wholeheart-
edly.

George W. Bush eventually became the president. President
George W. Bush was literally cruising after the 2000 presidential
election was called in his favor. He was cruising until September
11, 2001 when terrorists wrecked unspoken and most horrible
attacks that killed more than 3,000 people at the World Trade
Center in New York City, 189 dead at the Pentagon because terrorists crashed a jet into the building. Forty-four on Flight 93 died
in the crash at Somerset, Pennsylvania. The number of dead and
missing at the World Trade Center has been constantly revised
downwards since September 11, 2001 but it's apparent about
3,000 died. The figure includes those who died at the World Trade
Center and those crashed-landed when the terrorists hijacked their
planes.

Certainly, it was not all joke for Dubya prior to September 11.
But it seems to me it was a lot of times. Right after his inaugura-
tion, he picked his cabinet rather quickly and almost all of them
sailed through the confirmation process rather easily. He received
mostly a favorable response to his choices. Many thought like he
promised during the campaign, that he was going to surround
himself with some knowledgeable and experienced individuals in
his cabinet. He did especially with the likes of Secretary of State
Colin Powell and Secretary of Defense, Donald Rumsfeld.

After picking members of his cabinet, it appeared to me Dubya
remained in his campaign mode. He traveled around the country
and continued to sell his $1.3 trillion tax cut. It was the same "It's
your money. It belongs in your pocket and not in Washington."
To which he received predictable applauses from his supporters.
Never mind he never explained the details of the tax cut. It was
sold as if every tax payer was to receive either $300, $500 or $600.
He never mentioned some tax payers will not receive as much. He
certainly did not discuss or dwell upon the top one percent in the

population who received the largest share of the tax cut. Even some in the one percent indicated they did not want the tax cut. He pushed it through anyway. It was still like a joke. The joke continued until after September 11 and then we quickly learn that the surpluses have turned into deficits. Reasons given include a slowing economy and September 11. But September 11 has less impact than the declining economy and spending in Congress. Hardly mentioned as a reason for the deficits by the Bush administration is the $1.3 trillion tax cut. Many in the opposing party and others disagree. They blame the tax cut partially for the disappearing surplus and the emerging deficits.

Prior to September 11, 2001 and in fact in the summer (July) of 2001, some Republicans (and others) were very concerned about the president and the direction he was leading the nation. For example, there were mounting criticisms of the president's top adviser, Karl Rove. According to the July 2, 2001, issue of the New York Times, "Many prominent Republicans who once marveled at the Bush administration's agility say the president's lieutenants are increasingly stumbling in ways that are not merely embarrassing but also perilous to Mr. Bush's political standing."

Earlier on June 21, 2001 a New York Times article by Richard Berke and Janet Elder noted that "Despite his first overseas trip as president and the passage of his sweeping measures to cut taxes, President Bush's standing as a leader on both domestic and foreign fronts has diminished considerably..."

So it seemed like it was all a joke until the terrorist attacks of September 11 turns things around. Fighting terrorism became the president's top priority outdistancing other important issues like education, the environment, social security, health care and prescription drugs, and so on. Not only did fighting terrorism become the president's top priority and obsession, the fight against the Taliban, Al-Qaeda and the terrorists also meant infringements and even disregard to some of the civil liberties that Americans have come to be accustomed to. It did not matter. President Bush kept pushing forward bolstered by an astonishing high poll numbers close to 90% in support of his actions in Afghanistan. He capitalized on the high poll numbers and used it to set some laws by executive orders without going through the Congress.

This book is mostly a compilation of some of the articles I wrote in the past two years. It goes to illustrate that although the president has the reputation of a jokester, the American presidency and the duties required of that office are no jokes. George W. Bush won the presidency in an unforgettable manner and in the closest of American presidential elections. The controversy continues but there is only one president at a time and George W. Bush is it at the moment. Interestingly, former vice president Al Gore won the popular votes by more than 540,000 votes but losing the electoral vote in Florida cost him. Forget Florida. If he had won his own state of Tennessee, Florida would not matter.

I noted my observations with lots of supporting documents or news items from various sources including the New York Times, Washington Post, Washington Times, BBC World News, USA Today, ABC News, Reuters, Associated Press, National Public Radio (NPR), CNN, C-SPAN and others. This is not a book against President George W. Bush. Rather, it is a book about the observation made of a man that reached the pinnacle of the American and world power in spite of his perceived weaknesses such as his abilities to communicate his ideas, his lack of depth as in not giving much if any details of his plans and his lack of experience in legislation and federal government compared to Al Gore.

I thought it fits at this point to illustrate one of the reasons Mr. Bush has the reputation of a joker or someone that cannot be taken seriously. It is in his use of the English language. Some have referred to it as "Bushisms". Those familiar with some of the Bushisms will recognize them immediately. Here are a few examples from Bushcartoon.com. Quote, 'For every fatal shooting, there were roughly three non-fatal shootings. And, folks, this is unacceptable in America. It's just unacceptable. And we're going to do something about it.' 2. 'Whatever it took to help Taiwan defend theirself.' 3. 'First, we would not accept a treaty that would not have been ratified, nor a treaty that I thought made sense for the country.' 4. 'I know how hard it is for you to put food on your family.' 5. 'I know the human being and fish can coexist peacefully.' 6. 'I understand small business growth. I was one.' 7. 'The most important job is not to be governor, or first lady in my case.' 8. 'It's important for us to explain to our nation that life is important. It's not only life of babies, but it's life of children living in, you know, the dark dungeons of the internet.' 10. 'I'm a uniter not a divider. That means when it comes to sew up your chest cavity, we use stitches as opposed to opening it up.'

Those who may easily be offended because some of the president's gaffes are noted in this book need to realize that president Bush himself has made fun of his own gaffes and speaking style on more than one occasion. I recall he once said (paraphrasing) that he has been known to murder one or two syllable himself. The March 25, 2001 edition of BBC News noted that "President George W. Bush has poked fun at his own tendency to make verbal gaffes, or "Bushisms", at an annual meeting with Washington's journalists. During his first appearance at a Gridiron Club dinner, Mr. Bush said he suffered from foot-and-mouth disease and talked of cloning Vice-President Dick Cheney so he could take the next four years off.

Besides his unique use of the English language, President Bush who during the 2000 presidential campaign tried to give the impression that he understands and speaks Spanish very well was soon tested on his understanding of Spanish on his first official visit to Spain in June 2001. According to the Telegraph.com (June 13, 2001), while preparing to visit Spain, "He launched into shaky Spanish in an interview with Spain's state-funded television service broadcast hours before his arrival. In the event it was good enough for the report to conclude that Mr. Bush was the first Spanish-speaking president of the United States. However, change of language did not spare Mr. Bush from making the sort of gaffes that his opponents lampooned throughout his presidential campaign. He mispronounced the name of the Prime Minister, Jose Maria Aznar, calling him 'Anzar' but sounding more like ansar, the Spanish for 'goose'. Even as this book was about to be forwarded to the publishers, President Bush was still perpetuating his image of someone you cannot take very seriously with his reported fainting episode or collapse after swallowing a pretzel. Fortunately he is fine but the story is serious and funny and it's hard to hold back laughter thinking about the story. Incidentally, the bruise on one side of the Presidents's face looked like he had been in a fight with more than a pretzel. So the jokes continue but the presidency itself is not a joke.

For this book, I selected a lot of articles I wrote in relation to jokes and gaffes as relates to Mr. Bush and a number of articles dealing with character. During the 2000 presidential campaign, Mr. Bush and his supporters claimed to be 'the good guys' and painted Mr. Al Gore as a liar and a man of poor character. Well, that caused me to take a closer look at Mr. Bush with regards to his character. Essentially, his claims and portrayal of himself as the one you can trust to keep his words brought him closer scrutiny.

I disagree with many of President Bush's policies but there is nothing personal as far as I'm concerned with my criticisms of his policies or plans. In fact, I refer to my criticisms of his policies as "constructive" because I do not simply criticize, I offer my own suggestions or solutions to counter the perceived problems.

I thought about and concluded on the title of this book long before September 11, 2001. The terrorist attacks on that day jolted the nation and the world. With the exception of those who lost family and loved ones on September 11, no one in my estimation has been jolted as much as the president. Now he must act and he has with the pursuit of terrorist enclaves in Afghanistan and elsewhere. The president who for the most part was cruising along with a one month vacation after seven months in office suddenly found himself in a very serious and Horrible deadly situation. The jokes subsided though not entirely. Some of the smirk have been taken off his face but there are still some left. But as the 'war' in Afghanistan nears to an end, 'Dubya' and his White House appear somewhat confused in my estimation about what's next or who's next. Iraq, Libya, Somalia, Lebanon or where? In his latest (2002) State of the Union speech, he described Iran, Iraq and North Korea as "axis of evil.' That has raised a lot of eyebrows around the world and even some of the American allies in Europe and elsewhere question that characterization. The tricky thing about terrorists is that they are all over the world including right here in the USA and within the borders of America's closest allies such as Britain, Italy, Germany and Saudi Arabia. Getting rid of terrorism is not an easy task and the president knows that. For example among the three members of the captured and imprisoned Taliban soldiers are three former Taliban soldiers who claim to be British. Not only is that a source of embarrassment for Britain, I do not anticipate America attacking Britain because of the three Taliban British soldiers. Ironically, there is an American-Taliban (John Walker) whose case was referred to the civilian court rather than the military tribunal for trial.

Affirmative Action

Supporting 'Dubya' on this one

In keeping with my pledge to write in support of Dubya if he or his administration does what I like, here's another example. I support affirmative action and I'm glad the Bush administration choose to back an ongoing case in support of affirmative action in Colorado following a court action filed by a white-owned company at the Supreme Court.

I'm glad Dubya and his administration came out in support of affirmative action in this case. This has upset many of those who oppose affirmative action including Linda Chavez whose appointment by president Bush as Labor Secretary was derailed by her failure to report an illegal nanny she employed

As usual, I'm curious to see or read what right-wingers and Bush supporters and those against affirmative action think about the decision of the Bush administration to support affirmative action this time.

Finally, I think that the administration's latest action to back affirmative action in the Transport Department case is another illustration of what I predicted before. I indicated that Dubya and his administration will try to move away from the hard right positions it has been taking as in tax cuts and missile defense. I predicted it will look for issues that will put some compassion into his "compassionate conservatism".

President Bush's political decision to support stem cell research is one of those 'move to the left or to the center" issues. Supporting affirmative action is another. It is also good politics because I do not think the administration wants to anger a few of the minorities that support them. I also think the administration had to support affirmative action in this case because the Secretary of Defense Colin Powell is a strong supporter of affirmative action.

The Black/Latino Vote

Gov. G.W. Bush (Dubya) Seeks Black Vote: It's A Joke 'Cause He's Not Serious About It

Gov. G.W. Bush, affectionately called Dubya by me is seeking black or African-American votes. Given that Dubya is the national leader of the Republican party and their choice for the presidency, it is logical to add that Republicans are seeking African-American votes. Forget about it. It is a joke. They are not serious about it. Just talking about it and lip service will not do. Dubya and Republicans must show concrete steps or plans that address issues of concern to African-Americans.

Embedded in the last sentence above is a fundamental problem for Dubya and Republicans. A lot of Republicans want to deny there are specific problems facing blacks that need to be addressed and resolved. They see any effort to improve the conditions of African-Americans as special treatment or favor. They rather bury their heads in the sand than discuss the issues and solutions or potential solutions to the problems. Right of the mark, many of those individuals find the word "African-American" aggravating. They condemn those who use the word without any appreciation, respect or regard to those blacks who choose to use the hyphenated word. To many of such individuals, what we have is American problem. Sure it is American problem but there are some American problems that are of most concern to African-Americans. Once again, and for those who worry too much about the use of the word "African-American", the word is used as a matter of cultural/ethnic heritage and pride. It is not a rejection of America or Americanness.

Unlike other Americans who can trace their countries of origin or that of their parents, grand parents and great grand parents, most African-Americans cannot do that because their ancestors were enslaved. Therefore they attach Africa to America to reflect the origin of their ancestors. Why anyone will be bent out of shape about that is beyond me. References to Italian, Irish, German, Mexican, Cuban, Norwegian, Swedish American etc is fine with the same individuals and do not draw instant condemnation from them. It should not in my opinion. It is about cultural and ethnic pride.

Gov. Bush appeared at the N.A.A.C.P convention yesterday. He is in search of black votes and he learnt some lessons from his previous mistakes and the mistakes of former Republican candidate, Mr. Bob Dole. Mr. Dole turned down the invitation from the civil rights group in 1996. He thought it was a set up. In July 1999, the two democratic candidates in the primaries accepted an invitation to speak to minority (6,000 of them) journalists in Seattle. None of the Republican candidates responded until Dubya and Sen. McCain read an article in Los Angeles Times critical of their absence. (Michael Fletcher, Washington Post, July 9, 1999). Suddenly, the two Republican candidates found time on their schedules to make quick appearances. Dubya was incidentally campaigning in Seattle, the same city hosting the convention. He appeared for 15 minutes but did not take questions from the audience. Very typical of Dubya.

Senator McCain flew into Seattle after reading the LA Times article. He declined an earlier invitation to appear at the conference. He said "he favors affirmative action and absolutely and unequivocally committed to appointing an Asian-American to his cabinet..." (W. Post, July 9, 1999)

So Dubya learnt his lesson and showed up at the ongoing 91st N.A.A.C.P. 2000 conference. I'm glad he showed up. Did he change any minds? That's another question. To answer my question, I doubt if he changed any minds. My doubt originates from the fact that he said nothing that will bring some of the votes he is seeking. As usual, he was not specific. He did not take any questions as he normally does. Is the man scared someone will ask him a question or questions he could not handle. He made general statements and was simply vague. I thought one of the participants at the conference put it best. Other people (like me) are able to see through all the fluff that Dubya presented.

He (Dubya) received a few cheap applause with statements like "...strong civil rights enforcement will be a corner stone of my administration." Okay, but who in America believes that Dubya will enforce civil rights laws more than president Clinton or VP Al Gore? I applaud Dubya for at least recognizing that "discrimination is still a reality even when it takes different forms..."

Dubya missed an opportunity to attract maybe a few more black votes yesterday. He failed to capitalize on his opportunity. Rather than touch or address some of the issues that concern blacks specifically such as the death penalty, affirmative action, support for public schools/education, expansion of hate crime laws, the confederate flag in S. Carolina, high crime rates/guns in inner cities, police brutality, unfair jail time for drug offenders, increase in minimum wage, etc, Dubya slipped right back into his scripted notes on education improvements in Texas without mentioning "vouchers" because he knew his audience.

Dubya is repeating the same mistakes Republican candidates made and continues to make. My sense of it is as long as Dubya and the Republicans continue to deny there are specific issue of concerns to blacks, most blacks or African-Americans will continue to deny them of their votes. It is simple. They will support other candidates (mostly Democrats) who listen to their concerns, speak to their concerns and work with them to find solutions. I get weary of many Republicans especially their leaders and mouthpieces who blame civil rights leaders as misleading African-Americans. It is as if the people themselves do not have a mind of their own. They do. Contrary to what the Republican mouthpieces say they (African-Americans) know who is on their side and do not need the likes of Revs. Jesse Jackson, Al Sharpton, and Mr. Kweisi Mfume to tell them who to vote for.

Finally, if Republicans continue with their old and current ways of denials and neglect with regard to issues confronting blacks, they have nobody but themselves to blame for their inability to attract black votes. They can point to a handful of blacks such as Rep. J.C. Watts, Gen. Colin Powell, Dr. Alain Keyes, Justice Thomas and Dr. Condelezza Rice. Maybe they figure that's all they need to win.

Beyond Pandering to the Hispanic/Latino Votes

This was one of the articles I wrote during the 2000 presidential campaign.

Bush (Dubya) and Gore are pandering to the Hispanic/Latino voters. But beyond the pandering, one (a voter) needs to examine which one of the candidates or which one of the two major parties (Democratic or Republican) have done more to support Hispanic causes and concerns. That's what matters to me and so we must examine the issues and the records to see which party is friendlier to Hispanics and Latinos.

I bet some people thought or think that Dubya speaks Spanish better than Gore. Both speak some Spanish. Nonetheless, beyond speaking the language, photo-ops, dancing to tunes by Ricky Martin or Carlos Santana, eating some tacos or nachos with potential Latino voters, wearing Latino-like western wear, mariachi suit or 5-gallon sombrero are the more important issues that matter and the past records of the political candidates and parties.

Which of the two parties and the two candidates are in favor of Affirmative Action? Generally Dubya and the Republicans are not in favor of Affirmative Action.

The Latinos are concerned about other issues that face Americans including education, health care, social security and the environment. In addition, they are more specifically concerned with immigration issues, improving the minimum wage and the debate (especially in some states) about mono and bi-lingual education with respect to English-only or both the teaching of English and Spanish in schools. It is no secret that most Latinos identify with Democrats more on the issues that concern them. There are a lot more Hispanic/Latino officials who are Democrats than are Republican Hispanic/Latino officials. In the upcoming Republican convention, check out how many Latinos involved compared with those you will find in the upcoming Democratic convention. Is not even comparable because there are a lot more in the Democratic Party. Republicans (as in explaining why most blacks vote Democratic) will probably blame it on Hispanic and Latino leaders and the "liberal press." "Liberal press"? Don't get me going on that!!

So beyond all the pandering, Latino voters know who is pandering the most based on personal records and the records of the two major parties. Latino voters will vote based on their past experiences and the records of the individuals and parties seeking their votes. Which of the parties for example will put qualified (and there are a lot of them) Latinos (including judges) in top positions more than the other party?

Republican Campaign Tricks

Caught In The Act: Republican Dirty (Very Dirty) Tricks Exposed

Gov. G.W. (Dubya) Bush seems to have ran out of ideas. He did a long time ago. He never had much ideas in the first place. The Republicans (in Congress) seems to have ran out of ideas. They proved it long ago with the title of a "Do-nothing" Congress. The Republican National Committeee (RNC) seems to have ran out of ideas also. They just had a commercial to prove it.

Their bankruptcy of ideas nothwithstanding, the Republicans still want to win the presidential and congressional elections by all means including very dirty tricks like negative false advertisements. Well, they were caught in the act this time. The negative advertisement the RNC was about to air was pulled at the last minute. Television stations are showing it anyway but not as an advertisement. Pulling the advertisement has split the Dubya camp because according to the New York Times, "...some of his advisers had argued that the party should run the advertisement..." More about those advisers in a minute.

The commercial was so far out of line that Dubya objected to it at the last minute. It showed an interview from six years ago where Al Gore said President Clinton never lied in his political career. Al Gore was responding to Lisa Myers (NBC News) about a statement Gore made about Oliver North who was running for senate in Virginia at the time. The exchange about North was not included in the commercial. The RNC wanted to remind the voters about Monica Lewinsky and Clinton and once again their attempt exploded in their face. Again, these people never seem to learn their lesson. They just do not know how to bring in Monica into the campaign because they are scared most voters will scold them for it.

What about those who insisted on running the commercial including Dubya advisers? Are these not the same people who question Gore's and Clinton's credibility? Are they not the same ones who claim moral purity? Are they not the same people who claim to be christians and decent human beings? Are they not the same people who claim to know God and Christ better than the rest of us? What a bunch of hypocrites!!!

Finally, I told you Dubya and his supporters are still dazed following the Democratic convention and following Gore's rise in the polls. Gore is looking better everyday and the blunder by the RNC makes him look even better. Besides the RNC blunder, Gore is looking better because he is the one with a wealth of workable/practical and reasonable ideas. For example, yesterday in Maryland, he outlined plans for college tuition credits and new college savings accounts for taxpayers. The tax credit and savings plan are geared towards families earning less than $100,000 annually—the middle-class families. Gore has the ideas. There's plenty left where that came from. Meanwhile, Dubya and the Republicans are devoid of workable and reasonable ideas. They think they can win or deceive voters with negative commercials. They pulled one commercial but have promised to run other negative commercials in the future. According to the NY Times, August 25, 2000, "Bush campaign officials and outside advisers said the campaign had every intention to run commercials that could be defined as negative. But they insisted they have not settled on when..." If they think negative advertisements will cover up for their bankruptcy of ideas, they are deceiving themselves. Americans (most voters) know better than that. They cannot be bushwacked.

Videogate and Lettergate: I Smell a Rat, No, I Smell a Skunk

I have written about Dubya's line up of negative commercials which continue to backfire on the campaign. It does not quite stop them. Besides the negative advertisements, Dubya and his camp seem to have other dirty tricks. Take the case of the debate video that found its way to Gore's campaign. I have termed it the "Videogate". Gore's staff (former Rep. Tom Downey) who received the tape reported the matter to the FBI and resigned from his position. My gut feeling when I heard the news was that Dubya's camp is up with a dirty trick trying to create some sort of reverse "Watergate" with the election less than two months away.

I did not write about my gut feelings or what I thought at the time. I wanted the investigation to take its course because I did not (and still do not) know what actually happened. I write about this issue this morning because a suspect has been identified. The suspect, Yvette Lozano is employed by a media consulting firm that worked for the Bush campaign in Austin, Texas.

The FBI has a suspect but in fairness I still do not know what happened. I am fair and consistent when it comes to fairness. Stories abound of suspects who later turned out to be innocent. So as far as I am concerned, Yvette Lozano is innocent until proven guilty or until she admits any wrongdoing. So far, I smell a rat which is close to confirming my initial gut feelings.

I had a few reactions when the news of the debate video broke such as, "Who needs a tape of Dubya? What is there to learn? We have seen him stumble and mangle words. There was no advantage whatsoever in viewing a videotape of Dubya practising for the debates. All Gore needs to do is get out there and confirm why he is the best candidate among the two by showing his experience and comparatively detailed and well-thought out plans. He does not need Dubya's video." Those were the kind of thoughts that ran through my mind.

While I'm still giving the benefit of the doubt to Dubya's camp about videogate (until the investigation is over) here comes "Lettergate." Now forget the rat, I am smelling a skunk and it really stinks. This one is no allegation. It is another dirty move done and confirmed by the Bush camp.

Dubya says he wants to bring back honor and decency. He says he wants to run a positive campaign. If you ask him, he will tell you so not minding that he has been running a negative campaign compared to Al Gore. The 'RATS' and the other negative commercials support my view. The man who gives lip service to "honor and decency" has been running a negative and dishonorable campaign.

When will the "liberal" and conservative press (which may be one and the same) call him up on all that? There has been a lot of negative campaigning from the Bush/Cheney camp. I thought I smelled a rat. Forget that. I actually smelled a skunk and it stinks.

Yvette Lazano was later convicted.

Compassionate Conservatism

Compassionate Conservatism Is Still Very Much Right-Wing

We have heard so much about "compassionate conservatism" from Gov. G.W. [Dubya] Bush. He still has some difficulty explaining it and moreover convincing a lot of the voters what he means by that especially with all the 137 executions he has performed. It is also difficult to figure out when you examine some of his policies. Even many of his fellow Republicans especially in the right-wing initially objected to that concept and still have some difficulty embracing it.

Dubya is on his way to the Republican Convention in Philadelphia towing the "Compassionate Conservatism" phrase with him. He wants a "kinder and gentler" (his daddy's phrase) Republican party but no matter how he dresses it, the Republican party is still under the control of the right-wing. Compassionate conservatism is still very much right wing and far right in many instances. That's good news if you are right-wing but most of the country is not right-wing. By the way, I wonder how many people know that the term "compassionate conservatism" did not originate with Dubya. There is a reference to Vernon Jordan using that term as far back as the early to mid 1970s. Just wondering if people knew that.

So what is my evidence that "compassionate conservatism" is still very much right wing? You do not have to search very far. Dubya picked Dick Cheney who had a very right- wing voting record while in congress. The man blanketed yesterday's (Sunday) morning television shows. He tried to brush off some of those votes like voting against Clean Water Act, against the release of Nelson Mandela, against Head Start and against armor-piercing bullets. He said he might have voted differently on some of those today. He did not say which ones and the "liberal press" did not press him to indicate which votes he would change.

Mr. Cheney also said he was proud of his voting records as he has said on more than one occasion. On arrival in Philadelphia on his way to the convention, he once again defended his voting record and was adamant. He did not talk about changing any of those votes if he was voting today. So which one is it, Mr. Cheney?

Dubya's "compassionate conservatism" was used to soften the proposed Republican platform this time. The 1996 platform had called for the abolition of the Departments of Commerce, Housing and Urban Development, Education and Energy. Education too? I suppose they cannot do that this time since Dubya has made it a priority. There again is one place where right wingers clash with their priorities. A lot of them still want the Education and the other departments eliminated. They do not think the federal government should be involved. You do not hear them saying it out as loud as they used to because they know the majority of the country is against cutting off those departments. The GOP platform nonetheless is still leaning very much to the right.

The other reason to support the title of this article is illustrated by an article today (July 31, 2000) in the NY Times. Most of the delegates to the convention are right wing. According to the article, "On a host of important issues, from affirmative action to environmental concerns to abortion, the poll found that the delegates stand significantly to the right of much of the nation and even to the right of rank-and-file Republican voters. Dubya has similar beliefs. So where is "compassionate conservatism" in all of these? My answer is that it is absent and it is a phrase Dubya is using to confuse and pull one over the eyes of voters. Don't fall for that. I won't.

There is another point from the NY Times article I like to point out. I made that point more than once in my articles in the past. The article confirms what I have written with regard to the "big tent" claim of Republican leaders. The Republican delegates in Philadelphia represent the Republican party but it is not a true representative of America. The delegates are "...overwhelmingly white—almost 90%—and mostly male and middle age. By profession, they are more likely to be lawyers and business executives than teachers or farmers. They are relatively wealthy: one in five put their net worth at $1 million or more." Can you believe that? Is there any wonder the Republican party is out of touch with reality and out of touch with the desires of most Americans with regard to the policies they propose?

The GOP may have softened its platform under Dubya but it is still very much under the control of the right-wing. "Compassionate conservatism" is meaningless when you examine the heart and soul and the true beliefs of the controlling right-wing. The party has not really softened its positions on issues such as abortion rights, environmental issues, affirmative action and school vouchers.

White House Offices On AIDS and Race Relations: Open or Closed? Is this "Compassionate Conservatism"?

It was a blunder. There is some disarray at the White House. Who is speaking for the White House? Is it Ari Fleischer, Andrew Card, the president himself, the vice president, or who?

Some may have missed a major White House blunder. You can breathe easier because I will tell you. This story has taken a few turns in one day. Bush's Chief of Staff, Andrew Card's statement that "…Bush will not maintain two offices created by former president Bill Clinton: the Office of National AIDS Policy and the Office on the President's Initiative for One America…" I am convinced that Mr. Card would not have made any such statements if he did not discuss it with the president. He is very close to the president. He is so close he is the chief of staff. Well, shortly after the story was reported, there was instant outrage. Some blacks who just heard the news cried foul and so did some AID activists. Even a former Republican congressman (Steve Gunderson) reacted with "It sends a signal that AIDS is over, when nothing could be further from the truth." Further, he added that Bush's move "will probably be interpreted as negative about the Republican Party and the government generally." There was an instant outrage.

Fast forward to a day later. This morning, the Washington Post reported that "President Bush scrambled yesterday to defend his commitment to race relations and helping people with AIDS after his chief of staff mistakenly said the offices devoted to those issues would be closed…White House officials (and I ask again "Who is speaking for the White House"?) insisted Chief of Staff Andrew H. Card Jr. has been misinformed when he told USA Today that the offices, both created by Presiden Bill Clinton, would be shuttered."

What is going on? You mean to tell me that Andrew Card just spoke on his own without discussing the issue with the president? I doubt it very much. I expect this sort of self-inflicted confusion in a Dubya's administration. He is not a polished politician and he does not have valuable experience. Does anyone remember one of my predictions about this White House? Who is going to go first? Is it Andrew Card, Ari Fleischer or who?

What about Dubya? How did he handle the question? He was simply rattled and irritated based on the manner he answered the question. In another post this morning, I wrote about Dubya mangling through a brief session with the press during his photo opportunity session. Well it did not quite proceed as he would have scripted it. How about this Dubya-like answer as reported by the Washington Post (Feb. 8, 2001). A reporter asked, "Mr. President, could you tell us how it is, sir, that your chief of staff did'nt know what your plans were for the Office of National AIDS Policy and the President's Initiative for One America?"

My fellow readers and customers/visitors, check out this response from Dubya. The president responded, "We're concerned about AIDS inside our White House—make no mistake about it…And ours is an administration that will fight for fair, just law in the country. Last question!" What? Oh my!! Not only did he evade the question, he hastingly wanted to get away from the subject and he did. Does any of that sound familiar from the campaign? By the way I did not know there was "…AIDS inside our White House." Talk about Dubya and the way he mangles the English Language.

Finally, I surmise that Dubya was just about to give us another dose of "compassionate conservatism" with the closure of the AIDS and Race Relations offices. He got caught with an instant outrage from those concerned about the negative impacts of such a move. He was forced to back off but I believe we have not heard the last of that. He and his team are likely to shut the offices down or rearrange it somehow. Is the Office of AIDS and Race relations open or closed? Stay tuned.

Death Penalty

Gary Graham: Protesting, Kicking, Screaming and Fasting On His Way to "Texacution"

This is about the execution of Gary Graham. This is a very emotional case and those who claim to lack emotions (mainly conservative Republicans and supporters of Graham's execution) will be reading this at their own risk. If you are familiar with the American political scene, you will probably identify my point rather quickly. Many conservative Republicans including their mouthpieces on talk shows accuse Democrats and "liberals" as operating purely from an emotional base. They say so while denying their own emotions. Everyone has emotions. You cannot write, respond, speak or act on an issue if you lack emotions. Just impossible and I wish they stop lying to themselves.

I happen to believe that Gary Graham was wrongfully executed. Something in me tells me that that man was killed for a crime he did not commit. It is not just "something in me" but the available evidence of lack thereof of his execution. The man was screaming and kicking to his death. He refused to order the famous "last meal" but rather asked for Governor G.W. Bush and reverends Jesse Jackson and Al Sharpton to be his witness. The governor declined his invitation. The man reportedly shouted, "They are killing an innocent man tonight." He maintained his innocence until his death. He did not go quietly.

The Republican governor of Illinois put a temporary stop to executions in the state after it was discovered (by additional tests and evidence) that few of those on death row were innocent of the crime they were about to be executed for. It became an eye opener for the rest of the country. Apparently, not in Texas where the governor has indicated that all those executed under his watch and command deserved the death penalty.

It is not disputable that Graham committed several crimes (especially robberies) as a teenager. In addition, his lawyer was known to have been very incompetent. He did not call the witnesses that reportedly were with Graham the night of the shooting. Reportedly, he also thought his client was guilty even before examining all the evidence. Yes, he was incompetent.

In conclusion, I'm glad I finally had the chance to write about the execution of Graham. It was wrong in my view and it has been bothering me for sometime. No one should be executed unless there is ample, undisputable and clear evidence that the individual committed the crime. Some argue that Graham was given many chances through 30 or so reviews. I listened to a lady on C-SPAN in a call-in show. She lived in Texas and she used to work in the state's correction system with attorneys. She indicated that those reviews are simply formalities where no minds changed. That was her view and she expressed it strongly.

Finally, as we celebrate the 4th of July and America's independence, let's remember the victims of injustice and wrongful/mistaken identity that has also resulted to death at times. Their freedom and independence were stripped from them and it is up us to ensure that such incarcerations and deaths never occur again. All eyes are on G.W.Bush in Texas for the high number of executions and there are valid reasons for the attention. There is a chance that some of those executed in Texas (including Graham) were innocent of the crimes they were executed for. Check the state of Illinois and other parts of the country if in doubt. Unfortunately, it is too late for the dead to do something about such deaths but it is not too late for those of us alive to do something about it.

Character

DUBYA: He's Begining to Show His True Character

I wrote this sometime in late August 2000. I wouldn't write so much about Dubya but he presents me with so much material that I have little or no other option than to write about him. Moreover and sincerely, I write about him because I do not think the man is the best candidate for the presidency. America deserves better.

The 2000 presidential campaign is in full swing. The pressure is on and in less than one week, Gov. G.W. (Dubya) Bush has openly displayed aspects of his character that have essentially been under wraps to most people. Can he take the heat? Can he take the pressure? Maybe next time he voices the word "character", he needs not look beyond himself.

On September 2, 2000, I wrote about Dubya's approval about a negative advertisement against VP Al Gore (Refer to: Dubya: A Hypocrite Seeking to Win With Negative Advertisements). That article illuminated an aspect of his character. A day after telling high school students that "…politics doesn't have to be ugly and mean…and a system that downgrades people to bring somebody up", he launched a negative advertisement against Al Gore. This is from a man who yesterday in a campaign trail said "it's time to elect people who say what they mean and mean what they say when they tell the American people something…" He was referring to Al Gore but I think he should not look beyond himself. He might as well be talking about himself.

Prior to his campaign speech in Napperville, Illinois, Dubya displayed another aspect of his character. The man keeps topping himself. He made an indiscreet remark to his running mate (Mr. Dick Cheney) without knowing the microphone was picking up the comments. He whispered to Mr. Cheney: "There's Adam Clymer, major league asshole from the New York Times." That was not a presidential-like remark. Mr. Cheney responded, "Oh yeah, he is, big time." Their supporters cheered them on. But was that a proper thing to say about a reporter who was doing his job?

Apparently, Dubya did not like some of what Mr. Clymer wrote about him or his campaign. Poor Mr. Clymer. The respected journalist was being prosecuted for doing his job. Dubya did not apologize for his comments. Rather, he said, "I regret that a private comment I made to the vice presidential candidate made it through the public airways."

I do not know what Mr. Clymer wrote that Dubya resents so passionately. Journalists have a job to do and for the most part, they are fair. They write what they observe and the source of their articles are often from the campaigns themselves. I'm afraid what Dubya will think of me if he saw any of my articles about him and his (intended) policies. I do not care. I know I do not attack him personally. My articles are based on his actions and his plans for America.

Finally, there are hundreds or thousands of writers across the nation that Dubya will denigrate or cuss out if he ran into them. Mr. Clymer does not have to worry so much. He must keep doing his job as he has always done. The truth must be told. Let Dubya keep cussing if he wishes. He is showing his true colors and character.

Governor G.W. (Dubya) Bush: Another Sign Corporations and His Business Buddies Will Run The Country if He is Elected

I cannot and will not be distracted with all the noise and hoopla about the appointment of vice presidential candidates by Gov. Bush and VP Al Gore. It is an important story and expectation but I will continue to stress the record or issues with regard to the candidates especially Dubya's. This article reinforces the one I wrote before. It is a way to examine how the country will be governed if Dubya is elected as the president. From his current records and style, it is apparent that corporations and business interests that support Dubya (and vice versa) will rule. Let's examine my assertion this time from his environmental record.

A few months ago, Dubya indicated he will be environmental president if elected. It was laughable given his environmental record in Texas. I suppose he thought we, the voters will be satisfied and convinced to vote for him if he utters the word "environmental." Well, it is not enough for me. To be fair, I must indicate that the air in Texas was polluted before Dubya took office in 1995. The question is whether the air pollution (for example) has improved or gotten worse since 1995. Dubya and his supporters say it has improved.

So how does air pollution relate to business interests running the country under Dubya? Here is the answer as reported by John Mintz (Washington Post, October 15, 1999). In Dubya's Texas, "instead of demanding that industry clean up, environmental activists and federal regulators say, Bush's appointees have lightened the regulatory burden on Texas's dirtiest companies."

There is more than enough in Dubya's record that signal how he will govern as the president. I even have to cut out writing on this topic because it is more of the same corporate interests running the show. There is nothing wrong with involving businesses (as well as others) in making decisions but to hand over all or most decisions to business interests or corporations is ridiculous. It is ridiculous because they will look out for their interests first. The interests of the ordinary voter or citizen is very secondary to them. Dubya is running to be an environmental president. Yeah right!! Americans beware.

I had more than one title for this article. I could have called it Gov. G.W. (Dubya) Bush: Corruption under His Watch; Corporations and Business Interests Running the Show In Texas

"Getting to know G.W. II." I could have also entitled it "Dubya, He Will Do for America What He has Done for Texas—Let Corporations Run It."

Dubya has been rather successful so far in the presidential campaigns (including the primaries) by not really discussing the issues in depth but rather hiding behind the image, cliches, sound bites and empty phrases that he utters frequently. What about the issues? Well, what about it? That is my interest in the election.

Beneath all the hype about Dubya's lead in the polls, must be many of his supporters unsure about his chances of winning the election based on his handling of the questions the press ask him. I do not think the confidence of many or most of his supporters are as high as they would like it to be. Why? Just listen to the man discuss the issues. There is nothing much there. If I was one of his supporters, I will not be confident either. Just examine the man's record in Texas that he talks about so much. There is nothing much there to brag about contrary to the image Dubya gives. On close examination, you will find many maladies in different departments. Maladies that beg for transformation and positive change.

I will illustrate with examples from the Texas Housing Agency. My examples are based mostly on an article by John Mintz in the June 30, 2000 Washington Post. On a visit to a run-down section of Battle Creek, Michigan in April, Dubya indicated his commitment to making housing affordable for all Americans. How will he do that I ask? Well, he started with his own question, "How do we help every willing heart…own a piece of this great land?" How do you accomplish that Dubya? He did not say. Rather, he indicated "I've got some ideas." What ideas Dubya? He did not say. He has little or no idea if you ask me.

Look beyond the image and cliches and examine the issues closely. You will discover quickly that hundreds of thousands of Texans especially the poor and minority reside in squalor conditions. That is the reality in Texas. Dubya will probably go down there hoping to take care of the problem and demonstrate his compassionate conservatism by speaking a little Spanish and dance to a few tunes of Mexican music. Don't laugh. Okay, I don't blame you if you laugh because if you understand Dubya, that is the kind of solution he will present especially as he seeks their votes.

Correcting Dubya's Deceptions About the Military

With peace at home and abroad, Gov. G.W. (Dubya) Bush's harping on America's armed forces and its readiness is a weak campaign strategy. It's weak because, the Clinton/Gore administration have strengthened the military and they keep working to improve on it.

I like to know one thing. When will the "liberal press" and right wingers call some of Dubya's statements about the military what they are—deceptions. What about lies?

Dubya, Dick Cheney and their supporters give the impression that the military is at its worst condition since Clinton/Gore. That is a lie and both the Pentagon and the White House have tried to correct them on that. Those corrections notwithstanding, Dubya stays on with his deceptive message. As much as he hated to pronounce it, I noticed that recently, Dubya has admitted America still has the best and the strongest force on earth. Did'nt he know that before? I suspect he did but he was just searching for cheap political shots. He openly admitted after being scolded for what was obvious.

Dubya's statements yesterday again show him continuing with his deceptive messages. He said in a campaign appearance in Michigan, "Vice President Al Gore and President Clinton had neglected the the U.S. armed forces. The signs are disturbing: recruitment goals aren't being met, we're short of equipment, we've got military people on food stamps." Clinton and Gore did not neglect the military. There is some truth in parts of what he said but he is not telling people the real truth including how much the military has improved under Clinton/Gore. He is not telling people that the number of military personnel on food stamps are far less than they were during his father's administration and when Cheney, his running mate was the Defense Secretary.

According to a CNN report (Sept. 7, 2000), less than two hours after Dubya spoke, a pentagon spokesperson told reporters that Dubya was wrong on his facts. Other publications including the Washington Post and the New York Times reported reactions from the pentagon spokesperson, Mr. Bacon. The CNN report indicated Mr. Bacon as saying, "recruitment is on an upswing. In the last couple of months, the services have exceeded their recruiting goals."

Two more deceptive examples from Dubya and I quit on this article. On the issue of readiness during the speech yesterday, Dubya claimed a Navy ship had cut short training because of lack of fuel. The Navy said "…the ship simply finished early and returned to port to save money and give the crew a break" according to Mr. Bacon.

Here's another one. Dubya talks about military personnel on food stamps like it all happened under Clinton/Gore. Well, here is the truth as reported by the Pentagon's spokesperson, Mr. Bacon in the New York Times (Sept. 8, 2000) Mr. Bacon noted that "…19,400 service members, nine-tenths of 1 percent of the total, collected food stamps in 1991, when Mr. Bush's father was president and his running mate, Mr. Cheney, was secretary of defense. Today, 5,100 are on food stamps, or four-tenths of 1 percent of a smaller force."

Everyone (including right wingers) should be infuriated at Dubya's deceptions about the military. I do not count on right wingers to be infuriated because Dubya is their candidate. I just wish I do not hear so much about "character" and "truth" from them because Dubya appears deficient in both qualities.

Since I like to give the benefit of the doubt, I'm wondering whether Dubya is misrepresenting the facts because he is lying outrightly or because he is ignorant about the facts. I do not believe he is that ignorant about the facts. Even if he does not know, he has close associates and staff (including Cheney) who ought to know the facts. Are they all running away from the truth?

Finally, I like to express my views about recruitment and morale in the military. I wrote about it in details many months ago. I believe that to a large extent the military has a tough time recruiting because of the robust economy. Poor recruitment and part of the so-called low morale are mostly due to the booming economy. How many people will voluntarily enlist when they can enrich themselves quickly through various businesses including dotcoms? The booming economy has its negative drawbacks ironically and the military is feeling the effects in terms of constantly increasing the number of recruits.

Republicans Plan To Politicize The War: Nothing Much Else To Use For 2002 Elections

It's despicable. It's hypocritical. It's outrageous. It's deceitful and it's shameless. That's about as strong as I can put it. How many times have I written that with Dubya and his administration, it's not what they say but what they do? In fact in the past year, I took it up as a task to watch what Dubya and his administration says and what they actually do. I had to do that because Dubya and his supporters claimed all through the presidential election in 2000 that he was the trustworthy candidate and the candidate of decent and unquestionable character. Dubya and his supporters literally clobbered Al Gore and falsely pinned him as the 'bad guy', a liar and one with dubious character. It was only after Al Gore conceded the election (he won) that Dubya and a lot of the same Republicans praised him as a decent man. Go figure. Let me get back to the reason I'm writing for now.

Terrorists attacked American soil on Sept. 11, 2001 and killed more than 3,000 Americans. It was an incident that galvanized all Americans and a lot of the world against those responsible for such a dreadful attack. So America united to fight against those responsible for the Sept. 11 attacks. If there was ever a 'just war' in my book that was it. Personally, I may have disagreed with some of the ways the war was carried out but as for going after those responsible for the attack on America, there was no double mind about that.

George W. Bush happened to be the president when the Sept. 11 attacked occured. I strongly believe Americans would have rallied behind whoever was the president not withstanding the political party of the individual. So Dubya asked and received the support of most Americans and the world. He and his administration were grateful for the support and said partisanship has no role when it comes to the war in Afghanistan. The country united to fight regardless of political differences. It was the right thing to do.

Guess what? Now Karl Rove, president Bush's chief political adviser wants to turn the war to the political advantage for the Republicans.

Not that I'm surprised. How many times have I written that the president is using the war to his own political advantage. Again he did not ask for the Sept. 11 attacks but he has used the attack to his advantage by signing certain executive orders even to the detriment of civil liberties, obtaining almost whatever he wants from Congress and by injecting the war in his speeches in and outside Washington. Like I wrote before, he gets his loudest applauses when he talks about the war or America's resolve to hold those responsible for Sept. 11 attacks accountable.

Mr. Rove speaks with the president daily. I suspect he hinted the president about his comments before he expressed them at the Republican National Committee gathering. Just a suspicion but a strong one for that matter. How about Dubya speaking up to disassocite himself from Mr. Rove's comments if he means what he has been saying that the war is not a partisan issue? If he can do that, then he will be restoring some sense of credibility to his own comments about the war.

Clinton Destroyed The Military? What's Dubya Using In Afghanistan?

Just in case some people forgot, I thought I remind them of one of the major lies told by the Republicans in the 2000 presidential elections. Dubya Cheney, Republican leaders and a whole lot of Republican rank and file and Clinton/Gore haters hammered away all last year at how much Clinton had destroyed the military. You heard and read about it. They kept saying Clinton/Gore weakened the military to the worst extent. Never mind the lies and never mind their very selective memory.

I wrote a few times then about how Bush I and the then Defense Secretary Cheney really cut down the military. Right-wingers ignore that part just like they ignore major funding of the military by Clinton in his second term.

Anyway, this thought has been running around in my mind and I thought I put it down in print. If Clinton so destroyed the military, what's Dubya using in Afghanistan? The fighting men and women in Afghanistan just did not join the military since Dubya claimed the White House. They just did not start training since January 2001 after Dubya was installed either. Likewise, the bombs, the fighter jets and the aircraft carriers were not all built since January 2001.

I'm sure you get the point. Whereas a lot of the military armaments and weapons were constructed before Clinton, they were maintained in the finest of shapes and not 'destroyed' or 'weakened' by Clinton. Similarly, the fighting men and women carried on their training under Clinton in preparation for any wars that may come their way. Now Dubya has deployed the troops trained under Clinton and both the troops and the military fighting machines and ammunition are performing very well (for the most part).

I had to write this article to show how another lie we were told (some still tell the same lie today) is simply ridiculous and unfair. I had to write this article because no one (at least I have not heard) in the main press or the so-called 'liberal press' has had the guts to ask the president or Dick Cheney a very simple question that would expose them as lying to the nation during the campaign. That simple question is, "If Clinton destroyed the military like you charged, why is the same military performing very well in Afghanistan? I rest my case.

President Bush and His Administration: Total Lack Of Compassion and Clear Case Hypocrisy and Double Standards—Anthrax and AIDS Drugs

For anyone else who might be wondering why anyone or any country might dislike or hate America, here's another article that should grab your attention. Sometimes some people dislike or hate America because of a clear double standard or hypocrisy. I will illustrate with Anthrax and AIDS drugs and I will compare the number of victims killed by AIDS and those killed by anthrax (in recent weeks).

Prior to Sept. 11 terrorist attacks and the following anthrax scare, one of my major issues and concerns has been the devastation AIDs was inflicting in Africa (and around the world). More than 2.5 million people died of AIDS and AIDS-related illness in Africa last year (NPR, Nov. 5, 2001). Around the world, more than 22 million have died of AIDS and related illness.

What did Dubya and his administration do when a single person died of anthrax with the potential of other deaths (four to date)? The administration threatened and forced Bayer, the maker of cipro to cut down the cost. Bayer lowered the price of the drug.

Can there be a clearer example of hypocrisy and double standards (when you examine the cipro matter) than the Bush administration's refusal to allow for drop in prices for AIDS drugs and allowing developing nations to produce generic AIDS drugs? The hypocrisy is crystal clear.

To many around the world especially AIDS and other victims, they will probably be wondering if a single life in America is considered so much higher or more precious than a single life in Africa or the thousands that die daily from AIDS in Africa alone.

I really do not think most people around the world hate Americans. They don't. What I think they hate is some of the policies various administrations have supported or implemented in the past and present. Dubya's refusal to lower the cost of AIDS drugs or even support the developing countries to produce their own generic brands will not endear him to the hearts of many AIDS victims around the world and likewise such refusal will not endear him or his administration to the hearts of the family members and the loved ones of the victims of the disease.

Again, I aim to point out the truth and reveal hypocrisies when such occurs with this administration. I call it 'constructive criticism'. My views may not be popular but then I'm neither a politician nor am I running a popularity contest. The truth must be told regardless of who it makes uncomfortable. In fact, I wish most people can come out of their comfort zones and call for a national emergency and action about the ravages of AIDS here and abroad.

Separating Anti-Washington D.C. Rhetoric From Reality

If I hailed from Washington D.C., I would not like it. I am not from Washington D.C. and I still do not like it. I like to visit there whenever I can. Why do politicians especially Dubya and many Republicans speak of Washington D.C. as if it is a place of horror, hell and abomination? The reality is that those who speak evil of Washington D.C. are the same individuals who will do almost anything (as in the coup in Florida) to grab and keep power in Washington D.C. Some of those politicians arrived in Washington D.C. 20 or more years ago and are still there in Congress or working for a law or lobbying firm in D.C.

How about our Dubya who loves to speak about "getting out of Washington D.C." I understand he refers to the politics when he says so but his anti-Washington rhetoric does not match reality. According to Howard Fineman in Newsweek (August 15, 2001), "In fact, this ostentatiously anti-Washington presidency may oversee the most far-reaching expansion of the federal power since the heyday of the last Texan president who loved his ranch: Lyndon Johnson." I write often about watching what Dubya does rather than what he says. He is on a path to expand the federal government more than before. I thought rightwingers or conservatives like Dubya would fight against such increasing roles for the federal government. What about the rest of the conservatives? How come they are mum about Dubya's plans? I have an answer. They are quiet because if it works for Dubya, they can potentially hold on to power and more ironically, they would stay longer in the same Washington D.C. they like to denigrate. Go figure.

President "Dubya" Bush: Couldn't Convince Second Graders This Time

President Bush talks and really brags about his Texan origin and values. He tries to disengage himself from Washington D.C. but he is very much of Washington D.C. and has been around there since the days of his father's administration.

The president was unable to convince second graders he is not from Washington D.C. on a visit to New Mexico. All his talk about being from outside Washington D.C. notwithstanding, he was unable to convince the young students that he is an outsider from beyond Washington D.C.

In answer to the president's question, the kids answered, "Washington D.C." The president told them he is from Texas but apparently in spite of his well-known anti-Washington,D.C. rhetoric Mr. Bush was unable to convince the young second graders that he is from outside Washington, D.C.

Bush Administration Is Limiting White House Tours

I thought the White House is the peoples' house. I know it is. It is sustained by tax payers money. Moreover, thousands visit the White House daily but I suspect thousands more do not bother to visit. I have been to Washington DC so many times but I'm yet to take a tour of the White House. Why? I discovered in the past that I had to be in line as early as 5 a.m. or even much earlier to have a chance of getting in or picking up a ticket. I still would like to visit but it seems now Dubya's administration is making such visits very difficult. That has upset many in the tourist industry in Washington DC.

According to nytimes.com (May 13, 2001), a supervisor for one of the tour buses "…is not a happy man. He just cannot seem to get the tourists on his buses into the Bush White House.

In their defense, White House officials spoke about "trying to regulate and decommercialize White House visits." Many including some of the bus drivers simply did not believe the excuse by the White House. Likewise some of the representatives from the Washington, D.C. area did not believe the excuse.

Apparently, it seems I will not be taking my White House tour anytime soon. I was unable to do so in the past due to the time factor. Now Dubya's administration is making it even more difficult to visit. This administration has effectively managed to shield Dubya from the press and from answering reasonable tough or challenging questions. Now they are shielding the people and the tax payers from visiting their house.

The White House has gone to the Bushes! If this happened or was reported under Clinton, Dan Burton and the rest of the Clinton haters will be ready with their investigation and subpoenas by now. That is how ludicrous, crazy and investigation-minded those people were in the past eight years.

Our President Says, "No Child Should Be Left Behind in America": What Does Our President Do?

I do believe I'm doing my part. I consider some of my writings the least I can do to expose some of the hypocrisies of the new administration. In general, American voters have a very short memory and sooner or later but usually sooner, they forget most of the things "honest characters" such as Dubya says or said during the campaign. Presidential candidate, George Bush stealing directly from the Children Defense Fund's theme of "Leave No Child Behind", told us his administration will leave no child behind.

The president talks so much about not leaving any child behind. But what exactly has the president proposed in his new budget that is aimed to finance the $1.3 trillion tax cut? According to a Reuter's report carried by cnn.com (March 23, 2001), "Senator Hillary Clinton and other Democrats lashed out at President Bush Friday over proposed cuts in programs aimed at helping abused and sick children...Democrats said his budget would sharply reduce funding for child care and child abuse prevention programs as well as cut funding to train doctors at children's hospitals...They accused Bush of withholding needed funding for education, health care and other spending priorities in order to finance his $1.6 trillion tax cut package."

In defense, the Bush administration counters "that education department was receiving the largest percentage increase of any cabinet agency in Bush's budget..." The fact is that within the budget the president proposed are cuts that will hurt the progress of the children he claims he will not leave behind. The administration is increasing funding for education. It is also increasing funds for the National Institute of Health. I support and commend such actions but the truth remains that the administration is proposing cuts that will hurt the children they pretend to care for.

Dubya's Administration Makes A Quick About Turn Following Criticisms

Who says the president has the power to do anything he wants? That may be so but not when he gets busted while trying to sneak a policy behind us and through an organization like the Salvation Army under the disguise of "faith-based initiatives." Following lots of criticisms, Dubya and his administrations made a quick about turn pulling the rug right from under the Salvation Army leaving them wondering what happened.

According to the New York Times (July 11, 2001), "Although administration officials said around midday that they were considering the Salvation Army's request, the White House announced early tonight that it had decided to deny it..." Oh oh!

The Bush White House: Another Clear Evidence It Lied About the Salvation Army/Sexual Bias Issue

I told you I trusted the Salvation Army version of the sexual bias flap than the White house version. I told you the White House lied by denying the story. I told you the administration has been busted again lying. Just last evening, the National Public Radio (NPR) reported that the White House was blaming a lower level staff member for the flap. Poor staff member. The reality is that the blame resides further up the chain-way up.

Here is the clear evidence that Dubya's White House lied. And you wonder why I pity the likes of Ari Fleischer and Scott McClellan whose job it is to communicate official lies/misstatements which are shortly discovered to be just that-lies. According to the Washington Post (July 12, 2001), "Karl Rove, President Bush's senior adviser, was the Salvation Army's first White House contact in its effort to win approval of a regulation allowing religious charities to practice anti-gay workplace bias, administration officials said yesterday

Once again, where is the outrage from right-wingers who supported Dubya? Where is the outrage from the people who told us about the squeaky clean character of Dubya and his staff? Why are those who lied about Mr. Al Gore painting him as 'untrustworthy' suddenly silent with all the lies that emanate from Dubya and his administration? What Karl Rove did here at the least violates serious ethical rules. And this is in addition to his other ethical violations under investigation.

This most recent White House lie and embarrassment deserves an investigation. Rep. Jon Conyers is apparently thinking about one. He should and Democrats should stop fearing to investigate this White House just because, many will see it as a payback to what Republicans did to Clinton. I am of the opinion that Dubya and his administration must be investigated if they violate any rules. It appears to me they did this time. Dubya and his administration are not as squeaky clean as they claimed.

Dubya: The "Uniter and not the "Divider "Is Busy Doing The Opposite

Dubya claims to be a "uniter and not a "divider". Although "uniter" is not a word in my dictionary, I understand what he meant and I believe others understand what he meant too.

So how is the 'uniter' doing? I say he has been too busy disuniting and dividing not only members of his own party (Sen. Jeffords and his decision to pull out of Vieques which I support are two quick examples) but also America. You can now add Europe and the rest of the world to the list following his tour of some European countries. I knew and I have written he was not liked by many in Europe because of some of his policies like his views on Kyoto treaty, environment, death penalty, ABM, and missle defense. I can now write without a doubt that thousands of people dislike Mr. Bush in Europe.

I know that thousands of people dislike Dubya in Europe because of the thousands that came out to demonstrate against him and America since he represents America. How bad is the hatred. It is so bad some came out to moon him in Sweden. Even the New York Times (June 15, 2001) took notes. According to the NY Times, "at one point, dozens of protesters participated in a mooning-starting a countdown and then dropping their pants in unison.

Dubya, contrary to his rhetoric is showing how good he is at disuniting and dividing people. Sure he tries and attempts to invite some of his opposition to the White House for lunch or dinner. He wants to show he can work with the opposition. An observation I made is that he promises to listen but in most cases he does what he already has in mind.

Dick Cheney Is Back To Work And Doing Jumping Jacks!!

That's right. As most of us (politically inclined) know, vice president Dick Cheney with a chronic heart problem is back to work. I wrote about Dick Cheney yesterday. What caught my attention today is President Dubya Bush's reaction reported today in the Washington Post (March 8, 2001).

According to the Washington Post, "Bush told reporters Cheney is 'doing great' and 'feeling healthy.' He was doing jumping jacks today." "Doing jumping jacks"? That's great. That ought to reassure you about Cheney's condition. The denial and deceit continues.

Candidate Dubya Bush and President Dubya Bush: Double Talk and Flip Flops

Candidate Dubya Bush was cheered by millions of his supporters when he denounced the Clinton/Gore administration for sending American to Kosovo and elsewhere. His supporters and Clinton/Gore haters jubilated when he promised to withdraw American troops from Kosovo. He certainly got a lot of votes on that promise and other promises.

President Dubya Bush goes to Kosovo (as he did yesterday) and declares that "...America and its allies came in together, and we will leave together." What? What about the campaign promise? Not that I was or am in favor of that campaign promise.

Hello Dubya! What about your campaign promise of bringing them home immediately? To placate the troops further, he signed the $1.9 billion added to help their salary. That is another evidence that Dubya is not that stupid. The troops jubilated and probably forgot about the flip flop.

Where are all those right-wingers and Dubya supporters who were cheering for Dubya when he promised to withdraw the troops once he is in office? I notice they are all silent now. I don't see or hear any of them complaining about the lie Dubya told about withdrawing the troops from Kosovo. What a bunch of hypocrites!

President Bush Breaks Another Campaign Promise: Troops In the Balkans

I keep an eye on Dubya. I watch what he does and not what he says. I do this because I was fed up with how Dubya was being promoted during the 2000 presidential campaign by the press especially the right-wingers on hate radio and others. He was presented as a man of character and someone who you can trust. He also told us we can rely on his word because he does what he says. He and the rest of Clinton/Gore haters managed with the aid of a lazy and weak-kneed press to cast Gore as the liar and one without character. It really worked for them but I knew better.

Dubya just broke another one of his campaign promises. He castigated Clinton and Gore during the campaign for having American troops in the Balkans. He promised to pull the soldiers out if he became the president. I remember that so vividly that I do not need to quote a source for the statement. On a second thought, I decided to quote a source for the benefit of doubting Thomases.

I watched on the television during one of the debates in October 2000 when the former Vice President Al Gore called for extending the peacekeeping mission in the Balkans, Mr. Bush disagreed vehemently with "I hope that they put the troops on the ground so that we can withdraw our troops and focus our military on fighting and winning war."

That was from the same Mr. Bush I watched and heard on television say, "You will hear me say loud and clear in the Balkans: We came in together; we will leave together…"

That is a flat-out reversal of his position from his campaign promise. He now has taken Gore's position which he criticized during the debates to the cheers of his supporters. I wonder what those who liked his "Withdrawal" message then think of it now. Go figure. For the record, I supported keeping the troops there.

Analyzing Some of Dubya's Statements in Europe: Mixed Messages

This article is about some of the statements President Bush voiced on his European tour. These are not necessarily new. It is clear most European nations and most Europeans disagree with Dubya on missile defense, his plan to violate the 1972 ABM Treaty, environmental issues including his abandonment of the Kyoto Treaty and death penalty. They also have a concern regarding trade since Dubya has expressed his plan to protect U.S. steelmakers from foreign competition. Dubya is reminded about the opposition in Europe with hundreds and thousands of demonstrators lining up everywhere he appears.

During the press conference with Spanish Prime Minister Jose Maria Aznar, Dubya said, "Our intention is to make the world more peaceful, not more dangerous…" How can he do that when most people in Europe, European countries and other nations and people around the world are telling him they disagree with his plan to abandon the ABM Treaty. They also tell him they do not support his missile defense plans because it will lead to an arms race thereby making the world less peaceful. He did not have to travel to Europe to get a sense of the world's reaction or opposition to his plans.

In Brussels, Dubya said, "We must strengthen our alliance…" How does he plan to accomplish that when most Europeans strongly believe several of his plans will weaken the alliance? For example, in Madrid, in reference to the ABM Treaty, he said, "…prevents freedom-loving people from exploring the future…that's why we've got to lay it aside." When will Dubya realize the "freedom-loving people" he refers to do not agree with him. They do not want him to 'lay aside' the ABM Treaty. By the way is "lay aside" not the same as 'abandonment'? Of course it is.

When confronted with a question or statements he does not agree with, Dubya is fond of making statements like, "I will listen" or I'll give it a good listen." Whenever I hear that, it is a clue to me that he might listen but he either does not agree with you or he already has made up his mind to do something different. For example, in Brussels (BBC, June 13, 2001), Andy Card, the White House chief of staff indicated that Bush expects "a good listen." Of course he will listen but I suspect what he hears will travel out of the other ear immediately. Dubya is stubborn and inflexible with some of his plans. With such an attitude, no one should be surprised when others describe America as pompous and arrogant.

Finally, "In Brussels, Mr. Bush said he believed he was making good progress in convincing NATO members of the need for his controversial missile defense system." This is very easy to translate given all the opposition Mr. Bush is encountering. How about some truth? Sure there could be one or two countries or heads of state (like Aznar of Spain) that are listening to him closely about his plans, there is no doubt most Europeans oppose several of his plans vigorously. All the opposition notwithstanding, watch for Dubya and the White House to tell us how successful his trip to Europe was. I know better and so do millions of others.

The Cost of Pettiness, Arrogance and Denial

There are a lot of people within and outside the Republican party that are blaming President Bush and the Republican leaders in senate (especially Lott) for not taking Sen. Jim Jeffords seriously when the first signs (as in Vermont newspapers) reported he was thinking about leaving the Republican party.

I think I have already written about this subject enough but I wanted to add to the ones I wrote before. Mr. Jeffords indicated he was leaving because he was not getting along with the president and the Republican leadership on a lot of issues. He left the party based on his principles.

I listened (on television) to the president yesterday as he expressed his disapproval. I listened to Sen. Lott as he gathered the other Republican leaders after Jeffords defection. I think both the president and the Republican leadership are still in denial. The president says nothing will change and that he will push on with his agenda. Senator Lott and the Republican leadership said the same. They have not realized that the right-wing policies they are trying to force down our throats is costing them. The president forgets most of the voters did not vote for him. Therefore most of the voters are not too excited about his policies. He has not realized that yet. He still thinks he can "charm" his way through all his proposals. I do not see the "charm' but I do not want to digress.

The president lost Jeffords partly because of his pettiness for not inviting him to the White House ceremony for the teacher of the year who happens to be a Vermonter. It was not just his pettiness but also his arrogance and denial of the gravity of his actions. The Republicans probably do not need my advice but if they stay on the same tough-headed path, they stand to lose more than Jeffords. Already they have been warned by Sen. McCain and Olympia Snowe.

It's Official: Senator Jim Jeffords Bolts Away From A Party That Has Left Him

I was listening to Senator Jeffords over the radio as he made his announcement. At about 9:42 a.m. he announced he was leaving the Republican Party to become an Independent. He demonstrated in his statement why he is leaving the Republican Party. He essentially had enough of them and can no longer be a part of them because Dubya, his party and its leaders turned their backs on him.

Specifically, Mr. Jeffords noted some areas where he disagrees with the Republicans. He mentioned "choice, tax and spending, energy, environment, missile defense and education." In all those issues, Jeffords views are very similar to mine and most other Democrats. Mr. Jeffords declared he is "Independent" but in reality, he is a Democrat based on the issues and causes he cares about. Welcome home Mr. Jeffords. You suffered long enough in the other party.

So now the Democrats will control the Senate. It is still a very slim majority but it matters a great deal. Republicans can look at this change another way and I expect them to. They can now blame the Democrats for the inability of President Bush to get much accomplished. I did not think he was going to accomplish much in the first place even with Republicans in control of the Senate and the House.

Dick Cheney's Heart: A Topic Worthy Of Serious Discussion

I brought up the issue of vice president Cheney's heart problems during the campaign. I wondered if he could go the distance. Then my thought was mainly for the campaign. Since Dubya was selected for the presidency and now that Cheney has had another heart procedure, Cheney's heart becomes a subject worthy of some serious discussion. Well, I wonder how many Bush supporters and right-wingers that are nervous today about Cheney's condition but are acting like it is not a concern.

I think Dick Cheney is in denial about his condition. Dubya is in denial. Mary Matalin, Cheney's assistant is in denial. I even think that Dick Cheney's physician is in denial. Why is Cheney, Dubya, Matalin, his doctor and some others talking about Cheney's heart procedure and troubles as if it is equivalent to clipping toe nails? The situation is very serious but they have been in denial since last year. Stop the denial!!

Check this out. As serious as the situation is, Mr. Cheney says he feels "good". While selling his tax cut plan in Chicago in 2001, I recall a report where President Bush indicated he does not think Mr. Cheney should slow down or curtail his workload. He also indicated America needs Cheney's wisdom and judgement. There is no question that America needs Cheney's experience in Bush's administration. However, I think that when Mr. Bush says the country needs Cheney's wisdom and judgement, he actually means he needs Dick Cheney's wisdom and judgement.

The man (Cheney) should not have taken the job given the seriousness of his condition. The vice president replaces the president in case something happens to the president. Right now, it appears to me Dick Cheney should be thinking seriously about continuing in his current position with all the work assigned to him and the pressures that come with the workload. It is not too early for him to resign. He should take care of his health first. How much longer will he keep going like this. He should also think seriously about the country. Do we need a vice president who is endangering his health because of his workload and because of his weak heart? Maybe it's time for him to go and take care of his health.

Late night comics are have a lot of fun with Cheney's condition. I recall watching a "Mad" program on FOX several weeks ago on a Saturday night. They portrayed Dick Cheney collapsing with a heart attack with almost every statement he made. It was funny but in reality, it is not a funny subject. I think Dick Cheney needs some rest to take care of his heart. The denials must stop.

Dick Cheney's Heart: A Topic Worthy Of Serious Discussion

I brought up the issue of vice president Cheney's heart problems during the campaign. I wondered if he could go the distance. Then my thought was mainly for the campaign. Since Dubya was selected for the presidency and now that Cheney has had another heart procedure, Cheney's heart becomes a subject worthy of some serious discussion. Well, I wonder how many Bush supporters and right-wingers that are nervous today about Cheney's condition but are acting like it is not a concern.

I think Dick Cheney is in denial about his condition. Dubya is in denial. Mary Matalin, Cheney's assistant is in denial. I even think that Dick Cheney's physician is in denial. Why is Cheney, Dubya, Matalin, his doctor and some others talking about Cheney's heart procedure and troubles as if it is equivalent to clipping toe nails? The situation is very serious but they have been in denial since last year. Stop the denial!!

Check this out. As serious as the situation is, Mr. Cheney says he feels "good". While selling his tax cut plan in Chicago in 2001, I recall a report where President Bush indicated he does not think Mr. Cheney should slow down or curtail his workload. He also indicated America needs Cheney's wisdom and judgement. There is no question that America needs Cheney's experience in Bush's administration. However, I think that when Mr. Bush says the country needs Cheney's wisdom and judgement, he actually means he needs Dick Cheney's wisdom and judgement.

The man (Cheney) should not have taken the job given the seriousness of his condition. The vice president replaces the president in case something happens to the president. Right now, it appears to me Dick Cheney should be thinking seriously about continuing in his current position with all the work assigned to him and the pressures that come with the workload. It is not too early for him to resign. He should take care of his health first. How much longer will he keep going like this. He should also think seriously about the country. Do we need a vice president who is endangering his health because of his workload and because of his weak heart? Maybe it's time for him to go and take care of his health.

Late night comics are have a lot of fun with Cheney's condition. I recall watching a "Mad" program on FOX several weeks ago on a Saturday night. They portrayed Dick Cheney collapsing with a heart attack with almost every statement he made. It was funny but in reality, it is not a funny subject. I think Dick Cheney needs some rest to take care of his heart. The denials must stop.

Dictatorship

Reminding Dubya He Cannot Be The Dictator He Wants

During the 2000 presidential campaign, Dubya joked of being a dictator. He followed his uncomfortable statement with a nervous smile. I wrote about it then. In some ways since his selection, Dubya has tried to rule like a dictator. Need an example? You don't have to look too far. In my opinion, he has handled the American press like a dictator. How? The White House press is usually given a very short notice at the rare occasions he addresses them. When he talks to the press, he answers the questions as briefly as possible. There is no serious demand for a follow up. When that happens, he glides away with a "next question" pointing to a different journalist.

Do you need additional examples? How about Dubya acting and pursuing his rightwing interests and practically isolating himself and the USA from the rest of the world?

Well, this is America and dictatorship is not allowed or looked at kindly. The Senate and the GAO have moved to extract certain information from Dubya and his administration. The administration refused to supply some of the information until now.

I and millions of others are keeping a close watch on this administration. They ran their campaign and presented themselves with a holier-than-thou attitude. I know how much some in this administration and certainly many of their supporters thrashed Hillary Clinton and the Clinton administration for not releasing the names of those involved in the health care task force. They also thrashed the previous administration for 'stone walling' and not releasing certain information. The truth is that no amount of documents released by the Clinton administration would have satisfied the detractors. They were on a witch hunt. So why did I mention that? The Bush administration promised to be different. They promised 'a clean slate' and with only seven months in office, we see dirty slates here and there in the White House. They are not as clean as they claimed or as they would want us to believe. They are actually holding back information prompting the very rare GAO 'demand letter' (for example).

In conclusion, actions by the Senate, Congress and the GAO must remind Dubya that America does not tolerate dictatorship. If he thought he could become one in Washington DC, he should think again. Washington DC is not the same as Austin, Texas just in case Dubya thought he could get away with things he got away with in Texas.

Economy/Tax Cuts

Tax Cuts: Now That Your $300 or $600 Is In The Mail....

This article is about the ultimate in feel good politics which is what I think about the checks in the mail, courtesy of Dubya's tax cuts. Now that your $300 or $600 is on its way to you (assuming you are getting one of those) how do you really feel and what do you really think?

Let me answer my question first. Besides being the ultimate in feel good politics, it is another example of politicians seeking the easy way out rather than tackling the more difficult issues that confront this nation and the world. Sure, I can use $600 but what does that mean in the broader outlook of things. Is this not a clear case of eating now only to pay more in the near and distant future? Is this not another clear case where Republican politicians (for the most part) fail to learn from past histories including Dubya's tax cuts in Texas and how the state is suffering now financially because of it. The nation also suffered because of Reagan's tax cuts in terms of the enormous debts and deficits that resulted from it in addition to higher rates of unemployment and the deplorable conditions (economic and social) that America was subjugated because of his economic and other policies.

Some may think that someone receiving $600 should be excited. Sorry, I'm not. I would be but I know better. I would be jumping for joy but I think more about the long-term consequences and it is disturbing. I'm on record (as many others) for opposing such a large tax cut because it is based on projected surplus. It also favors a few in the population more than others. It rearranges the priorities and deprives money from areas that need it the most including education, environment, defense, energy, agriculture and others. In addition, I believe we should pay down our debts or deficits before seeking large tax cuts.

So I'm not so excited about $600 coming my way because I'm concerned that I will be paying more than that very soon in one way or the other to the federal government. Moreover, economic and other experts have indicated the tax cuts will do little to reenergize the economy especially since it is spread across ten years. Did Dubya sell us a lemon? You have to answer that for yourself but I think so.

Education

Debunking Dubya's Education Claims

I bet there are thousands or even millions of people especially the supporters of Gov. G.W. (Dubya) Bush who buy his rhetoric of educational excellence in Texas. Dubya has made it his most important priority (based on poll results). I'm all for education and I too believe it deserves the utmost attention and improvement. Dubya did not begin the educational initiatives in Texas but you hardly hear him give credit to those who started it. He has made it his own and taken it to a direction that even the originators may not have envisaged.

If you listen to Dubya, you will think that the state of education in Texas is unsurpassed in the country. Well, think again. It is not as rosy as he paints it. There are serious problems and there are a lot of critics.

Dubya never talks about the thousands of children that are forced to drop out of school. It is not a pretty picture. What about those kids? Apparently, they are not included in the "compassionate conservatism" mantra.

Finally, Dubya is promoting education in Texas. That's his right. The problem is that he is not telling the whole story. Some of the test scores in Texas have improved. The question is improved at what cost? When the totality of the programs Dubya is promoting is closely examined, he and the program might be doing more harm than good. His rhetoric on education may sound good and harmless but the results in the long run may be hurtful. Years of research have shown that to be the case. Hurtful. You will never know that if you listen and believe what Dubya and his supporters tell you. Unfortunately additional research into the issues take sometime and effort and not many people are willing to spend the extra time to find out the real situation. Some are just lazy and will not do additional research even if they had all the time in the world. Those are the most vulnerable to deceit and many sources including right-wing radio talk shows have done a good job deceiving them.

Education Bill: Several Right-Wingers Are Furious With President "Dubya" Bush

When I saw Dr. Bill Bennett (former education and drug czar under Presidents Reagan and Bush (Daddy) on television complain bitterly about Dubya's education bill and his apparent compromises (which several right-wingers hate), I knew then I had an article to write about the education bill. What is that will make several prominent right-wingers furious about their own president? I found several of my answers in the New York Times (May 2, 2001).

According to the New York Times, "...a number of conservatives in Congress complained that President Bush's signature campaign issue was being seized by Democrats and stripped of Republican ideas...and according to a Republican lawmaker (Peter Hoekstra of Michigan), ' this is no longer a George Bush education bill...this is a Ted Kennedy education bill."

Dubya is finding out how quickly some of his solid campaign promises are crumbling. Some of us notice but there are some who still think everything he is doing right now is just what he promised. No. Not at all. Besides, reality is taking over and even Dubya is becoming a "realist" on some of these crucial issues. So he was unrealistic about some of these issues even with all the warnings from the opposition? He has himself to blame for not delivering to his right-wing constituents. I'm not shedding tears for them. For example, "vouchers" have been thrown out of the window and Dubya has yielded on that. Good!!!

I wish the remnants of Dubya's education bill is totally a Ted Kennedy's bill as Mr. Hoekstra charged. One reason is because the Democrats also compromised according to Senator Kennedy. For example, the bill does not add more teachers to the classroom, renovate schools or expand after-school programs. I hope they find a way later to add all those because they are all vital to the education of American youths and the future.

Environment and Energy

Arsenic: After All The Noise, Dubya Adopts Clinton's Standard.

There were lots of exchanges on my website in the Spring of 2001about arsenic and Dubya's decision to seek a standard different from the 10 parts per billion (ppb) set days before the end of the Clinton administration.

I had quite a few of exchanges with Republican conservative visitors to the site especially with one staunch Bush supporter.

After all that noise and hoopla, Dubya and his administration decided to keep Clinton's standard. Once again, it goes straight to the heart of what I keep saying and writing about Dubya. Watch what he actually does and not what he says. I hope you remember him saying he was suspending the Clinton standard so he can arrive at a standard 'based on science and not politics.' It was a little cheap shot on Clinton and his administration. His supporters cheered on. Do you remember that? I hope you do. Now look at the standard Dubya is adopting. This one needs a little analysis and development.

Dubya came to power (and we all know how he got there) with a vow to overturn all that Clinton did including overturning the arsenic standards. So his fellow right-wingers cheered him on. In their mind, their political Messiah has finally arrived after eight years of the 'evil' Clinton. So right-wingers jubilated. Promising to reverse everything Clinton did was music to their ears. So on arsenic, they attacked Clinton for not understanding business. They shouted that an arsenic level of 10 ppb could only destroy business. Dubya's promise to reverse that standard was just additional ammunition for right-wingers and Clinton haters to denigrate Clinton further.

So what did I see last night in USA Today (Oct. 30, 2001)? It was an AP report which read "Reversing course, the Bush administration will accept a new, tougher arsenic standard for drinking water that was issued in the last days of the Clinton presidency." What? What about all those unfair Clinton bashing that ensued the moment Dubya announced he was going to seek another standard? Will all those right-wingers and Clinton haters now apologize to the man for all the rubbish they voiced about him? I know they will never apologize. They are certified Clinton haters.

So why did Dubya reverse course? Pressure was on. His record on the environment is terrible at best. The scientific evidence was overwhelming in favor of keeping the 10 ppb standard. Dubya was warned before he announced that he was going to review the standards not to do so given scientific evidence. He was warned by many experts including the respected National Academy of Sciences. He did not bulge. He was determined to reverse Clinton's standard. Now, after all those noise, rah-rahs and a bountiful of Clinton bashing, he reverses back to Clinton's standard. Look at all the time and effort spent arguing about that? I like to know how much additional dollars Dubya spent to have additional scientists look into the matter.

I argued then that the 10 ppb was right based on studies that go back to more than 20 years. Based on my research and readings, I actually suggested lowering the standards further. However, I accepted 10 ppb as a reasonable standard and compromise.

President "Dubya" Bush's Energy Policy: In Search Of a "Magic Wand"

Candidate Gov. Bush and his then veep pick (Dick Cheney told us they were going to fix the high energy prices once they get to the White House. Their supporters applauded and believed them. Some on this board really believed that the two oil men (having worked in the oil industry) will fix the problem once they were in charge. In one of the debates with Gore, Bush blamed the Clinton/Gore administrations for the high rise in energy prices. He spoke about how he would make the OPEC nations do his will by literally forcing them to reduce oil prices. He also spoke about domestic exploration and drilling.

In a previous article several weeks ago, I wrote about how Dubya suddenly could not do a thing when the OPEC nations cut production and consequently raised oil prices. It was left to Energy Secretary Spencer Abraham to express there was nothing he or the administration could do to stop OPEC from cutting production and consequently raising prices. Really? Apparently Dubya did not know that before he used increased oil prices to attack Clinton and Gore.

The reality is that things do take time. I was willing to allow Dubya some time on this subject but since he used it as a campaign issue and since he used it to win over some voters, it has to be disappointing that he and his administration just realized that it will take many years, well beyond his stay in office to resolve a reasonable portion of the energy crisis. That was not the impression he gave the voters during the campaign. I was not fooled but there were many who really believed oil prices will go down once Bush was elected because he knows a lot about oil. Energy prices may go down but is not because of the influence or the pressure Bush put on the OPEC nations.

How about this irony based on campaign promises? Oilmen Dubya and Cheney are now in charge but gasoline prices are at their highest and a possibility of a $3 a gallon in some areas is in the horizon. Reality has hit and what is Dubya's solution? Nothing that can help resolve the problem in the short-term and 'short-term' could be four years or more. Reality has hit and Dubya is searching for a "magic wand." There is none. He should have been honest with the voters about that during the campaign rather than leave the impression that he was going to take care of the problem immediately in office.

Dubya did not cause this energy problem. It is a result of lack of energy policy in this country for the past 25 years. I see Ari Fleischer put it as 5 to 10 years as if Clinton was mostly responsible for the problem. Earlier in his speech on energy policy in Toronto, veep Cheney blamed it all on Clinton.

Who is to blame for the high rise in energy prices? I place a lot of blame on the American people and their voracious appetite for gasoline and energy. It reminds me of the 'drug war'. As long as their is a high demand with those willing and ready to inject, smoke and inhale illegal drugs into their bodies, the drug war will remain a failure. For example, vehicles that get few miles per gallon are grossly inefficient energy-wise but people still buy them and no one will stop them from doing so. Simply put, some of the choices a lot of us make are hurting us energy-wise.

Who else is to blame? All the previous Presidents and Congresses in the past 25 years with the exception of Jimmy Carter. I know he pushed hard for conservation but a lot of people (especially Republicans) laughed at him and made fun of him for wearing sweaters near the fire place in the White House and for his promotion of conservation.

Oil companies are also to blame because there is clear evidence they are making incredible profits in the midst of the oil crisis. I place little or no blame on OPEC nations. In several instances, oil companies make more money or profits than the oil-producing countries themselves. In addition, the rest of the world for example do not ask the U.S. or the most advanced nations to cut down their prices on fighter jets and other military armaments they sell to those countries. The same applies to food and other products the advanced nations sell to the developing countries.

Kyoto/Bonn Climate Treaty: The World Moves On Without Dubya and the U.S.A.

Tell me again Dubya is not an 'isolationist'. He is an 'isolationist' on ABM Treaty, missile defense, Kyoto accord and global warming. That's the truth and Dubya supporters must deal with that truth.

Here is an example of isolationism. The rest of the world decided to move on with a climate treaty agreement in Bonn without Dubya and the U.S.A. According to BBC news, "In an historic deal, 178 countries have agreed how to tackle climate change."

In my opinion, the political Dubya I know would have loved at least one aspect of the Bonn agreement. He would have loved the Bonn agreement because the rest of the world struck a compromise. Unlike Kyoto, the Bonn agreement only required a reduction of emissions to 2% reduction in emissions (rather than 5% outlined in Kyoto) over the next 11 years.

Who is Dubya, the leader of the world's most polluting nation and the world's most industrialized nation going to call whenever he comes up with his own version of the Kyoto accord? Apparently, the rest of the world has left him behind.

Dubya Demonstrates His Hypocrisy and Deceit With His Energy Plans

Have you noticed gasoline prices have been rising recently. I thought our president and the vice president (Dick Cheney) were supposed to take care of that once they were installed. They were but gas or energy prices keeps rising. During the election, they gave the impression that they will resolve the problem immediately they get into office. I'm willing to give them more time because things are easily said than done.

Let's examine Dubya's plan to solve the energy problem and also examine some of his specific statements in that regard. His big plan is to explore and drill in the Arctic Wildlife refuge. Many environmentalists including Americans, Native Americans and Canadians strongly oppose that plan because of the impact on the environment.

Dubya also promised that he will more or less force the OPEC nations to reduce oil prices once he gets into office. Well, to the best of my knowledge, since he has been in office he has not said a single word publicly about OPEC or how he will get them to bring down oil prices. He has spoken about ways to explore for energy at home but nothing specifically directed at OPEC. I suppose he has realized there is nothing much he can do about OPEC. Even the Energy Secretary Abraham acknowledged that at one time.

Finally, how about this for contradicting yourself. Dubya indicated he will find alternative ways to dependence on foreign oil. So what did Dubya do in his current budget? He cut $190 million from funds that would be used in research for renewable energy resources in 2001. That's our Bush.

President "Dubya" Bush: Another Evidence That he Bows To Industries

I know I face the risk of sounding like a broken record but bear with me because my focus is on the issues. It is also about the truth. Dubya is on a roll. He is on a roll bowing to the industries and cutting back on environmental progress and conservation. This is another evidence that Dubya says one thing and does another.

No, this is not about his refusal to regulate CO2 emissions. It is not about his decision to pull out of the Kyoto accord. It is not about his decision to keep arsenic levels rather than follow a stricter standards suggested by the Clinton administration. It is not about his decision to withhold the results of dioxin in meat and it is not about his decision to cut funds used in exploring alternative energy.

This time, it is about his administration's plan to relax air conditioner standards.

According to the Washington Post (April 14, 2001), "The Energy Department yesterday announced the rollback of a Clinton administration rule mandating increased energy savings for central air conditioners and heat pumps in favor of a less stringent rule applauded by appliance manufacturers."

It sems to me that the Bush administration should have left the Clinton administration rule in tact if it cared about saving energy and reducing our reliance on foreign oil. On this issue of the air conditioner energy standards, I wish Clinton implemented it earlier. I fault him for not doing so because if he did and not wait until 2006, Dubya might not have had the chance to roll back the standards. Then again, the Republican majority at the time would have blocked or opposed it.

Environment and Public Health: President 'Dubya' Bush's Administration and Industries Are Holding the Country Hostage...Sort Of

Whether it is carbon dioxide emissions, arsenic, drilling in the Arctic National refuge, or discarding ergonomic requirements put in place by the Clinton administration, Dubya and his administration has shamelessly shown it is on the side of the industries. Again, this should not surprise anyone who knows Dubya. He is doing to America what he did for Texas in the area of the environment. I wrote about that last year.

There is no doubt that Dubya and the industries are kind of holding this country hostage at the moment with regard to environmental and public heath issues. This time, the chemical, beef and poultry industries are exerting their hold on Dubya and the nation. Scientists such as the one at EPA spend years and decades developing and concluding expensive studies. Dubya and the industries within split seconds dismiss all the studies because of their perceived influence of the industries.

According to the Washington Post (April 12, 2001), "The chemical, beef and poultry industries are waging an intense campaign to delay further an Environmental Protection Agency study showing that consumption of animal fat and dairy products containing traces of dioxin can cause cancer in humans..." health risk dioxin poses." As usual the industries are after their bottom line and any studies with results they dislike must be "seriously flawed."

Dubya bows to the industries because they have always backed him and the Republicans heavily during elections and campaigns. For example and according to the same Washington Post report (April 12, 2001), "The politically active chemical, livestock and meatpacking industries contributed $1,171,000 to Bush's campaign last year."

It is all about delaying tactics and profits for them more than a sincere dispute with decades of scientific report. Check this out. Some of the industry officials actually had a confession. W/Post indicated also that "Some industry officials concede their primary goal is simply to keep the study of dioxin--begun during the Reagan administration--going for as long as possible."

President "Dubya" Bush Tells The World--To Blazes With The Environment and Kyoto

I wanted to write this about four days ago when I first learnt that Dubya's administration has abandoned the Kyoto Accord that was negotiated by more than 100 countries. The treaty aimed at reducing greenhouse gases that contribute to global warming. Bulgaria happens to be the only country that has ratified the treaty but the other countries are diligently working towards the ratification.

I had just written about Dubya breaking his campaign pledge with the reversal of CO2 emission control and arsenic in drinking water. Those were all within a week. It is therefore not surprising to me that Dubya unilaterally pulled out of the Kyoto Accord. That was not only irresponsible, it was a clear demonstration of poor leadership. The USA under Dubya has lost any claims to be the world's leader in environmental issues and some other issues.

It was not just that Dubya pulled out of Kyoto, he did so without providing an alternative. There is no such alternative from the administration and what about this arrogance of doing as he wants and to blazes with the rest of the world? This is not a welcome news in many countries especially in Europe and Asia.

I heard all the excuses like, "Noboby else has ratified it" and "It (Kyoto) was not going anywhere anyway." Some are blaming developing countries such as China. How do you make the largest mess in the house and blame the youngest kid in the house for the mess? That's what I liken the blame to. The more developed countries (MDCs) in the world are responsible for about 85% of the greenhouse gas emissions. The USA is the largest contributor with 25%. The less developed countries (LDCs) contribute 14% of the emissions with China responsible for 9% of the 14%. How can any responsible person or country ignore the countries with the most pollutants and blame those that pollute the least? It is important to remind the LDCs to avoid the mistakes the MDCs made but the LDCs are really not the ones causing the most pollution.

China has actually shown lots of improvement in its emission controls. You hardly see that reported. I was glad to see the former EPA administrator in President Bush '41'administration, Mr. William Reilly, note the Chinese efforts in the New York Times (April 1, 2001) that "…China has actually reduced its carbon emissions over the past five years. The Chinese are certainly doing their part to clean up their emissions and I wish more people especially those in the current Bush administration knew that or expressed that fact.

Meanwhile, by Bush backing away from the Kyoto accord, the Europeans and others have expressed their outrage and they have used words like "irresponsible", "arrogant", and "sabotage" to describe the president's actions. (New York Times, April 1, 2001) Where is America's leadership? The world is asking but Dubya and his fellow right-wingers are telling the rest of the world to go to blazes. And we have four more years of this?

President "Dubya" Bush Bows To the Mining Industries: He Keeps Proving Me and Others Right.

You do not have to look hard to find or confirm this one. The environment is under assault by Dubya and his administration, Polluters are rejoicing and gaining strength daily because they know they have a friend in the White House. On arsenic, Dubya bows to his friends and supporters in the mining industry. Corporations seem to rule and control this administration and there ought to be no doubt about that at all. I wrote before he was selected as the president that corporation will rule if he gets to the White House. He keeps proving me right.

Just last week, Dubya broke his campaign pledge by backing away from regulating CO_2 emissions. The standard developed by the Clinton administration was not even going to take effect until "five to nine years." That still was not good enough for Dubya and his administration.

Scientists have found that arsenic in drinking water causes bladder, lung and skin cancer and other kinds of cancers and ailments

I have a simple test for those who wanted to lower or change the standards established during the Clinton administration. For the next four years, they should daily ingest water that has a concentration of 15ppb or 20 ppb arsenic in it. This must apply to all the water they drink. At the end of four years, they should be tested and evaluated to see whether or not the arsenic has had any effects on them. I guess they will not accept my suggestion but we can save a lot of time and money with such a test if they would become experimental guinea pigs. I just thought that if nothing is found to be wrong with them after ingesting that kind of water for four years, then maybe it is safe to eliminate the former standards and set new ones. It is very much like the analogy I apply in my Strategic Defense Initiative (SDI) test.

Just for those who are not familiar with my SDI test, I suggested that all those in favor of SDI should be placed in a very remote location like in Alaska. Then, the missiles should be directed at them while the rest of us observe to see whether they will be protected or shielded. To show our concern and compassion, only three sets of missiles should be directed in their location. If they are shielded from the missiles, then, the development and implementation of the SDI should be given a serious consideration. I might even have a change of mind about that. How about that for you 'arsenic-is-not-a-problem' and SDI enthusiasts?

Christie Whitman: Covering Up Dubya's Lies, Caught Herself Lying Too

It is known by now that President "Dubya" Bush lied and flip-flopped about his campaign pledge to curtail carbon dioxide emissions. So how did the EPA Administrator Christie Whitman handle the embarrassment after she assured Americans and Europeans that Dubya would curtail carbon dioxide emission?

Ms. Whitman defended her boss. It was not a very easy defense in my opinion. According to a CNN.com report (March 16, 2001), "…She said she didn't feel her advicehad been ignored, but understands the president is the one who makes the final decision…That's the way it works…' I guess so. The boss overruled.

I can only imagine how she felt. According to the CNN.com report, "…she assured European environmental leaders at a meeting in Italy two weeks ago that the administration would curtail carbon dioxide emissions." She said all that because she trusted the original pledge of her boss. How about that for trust and honesty?

Not only did Ms. Whitman defend her boss after the flip-flop, she caught herself lying in further defense of her boss but she quickly corrected herself. According to the CNN.com report, "…When asked by a student of the National Young Leaders Conference why Bush reversed his position, Whitman said: 'He didn't…Well, he did." Ouch!! She just could not lie about that again in front of those young leaders. She caught herself lying and pulled back.

Finally, Ms. Whitman indicated she will not resign now because she was reinforcing the president's campaign pledge while the president himself was breaking his pledge. Anyone familiar with my articles will remember one in which I wrote a few weeks ago (before anyone I know of) that different officials under this administration have been saying things differently from Dubya (and Cheney) positions. I wondered who will be the first to go because of it. Speaking about that, Scott McClellan seems to be featuring more and more as the White House spokesman. Is Ari Fletcher's role decreasing? You will recall I wondered how long he will be on his job. Covering up for Dubya and being less polished and experienced has its effects. It has to wear the spokeman out quickly.

President G.W. (Dubya) Bush Lied To Us About Reducing Carbon Dioxide Emissions

It is not uncommon for politicians to lie or to change their minds. It happens with politicians of all political stripes. This one is about Dubya and it is not the first time he lied. The annoying factor is the weak reason or reasons used to justify the lie. His father, asked us to read his lips and we did. "No new taxes" transformed into new taxes. His son (Dubya) told us countless times that he is a man of honor and character and that we can trust his words. Yeah right.

Is anyone keeping counts? How many of what he promised has he broken? How many of what he said have turned out to be false? How many times has he said one thing only to do something different?

The latest lie or deceit from Dubya should not really be a surprise. However, when you want to give someone a chance to prove himself/herself and s/he turns around and betrays you very quickly, it is very disappointing. That is the story of Dubya today. During the campaign, he knew he was no match to Al Gore when it comes to environmental issues (and a lot of other important issues for that matter). So what did Dubya do? He made a campaign promise he just broke. Where is the outrage? What happened to the man whose words are supposed to mean what they say? Dubya has again shown his true beliefs and has shown also that he is very much influenced by large industries (such as energy) and the right-wingers in Congress who oppose cleaner air and reductions in carbon dioxide.

According to the New York Times (March 14, 2001), "Under strong pressure from conservative Republicans and industry groups, President Bush reversed a campaign pledge today and said his administration would not seek to regulate power plants' emissions of carbon dioxide, a gas many scientists say is a key contributor to global warming." I do not think Dubya really believes in global warming anyway. I remember during one of the debates, he was uncertain about it but he faked his way through the question and answer session.

So what was the president's excuse for breaking his campaign promise? See if this was not as lame an excuse as you can find. I say so because most scientists conducting environmental and carbon dioxide studies have shown that CO2 is a primary cause of global warming. However, a primary reason the president changed his mind in imposing mandatory emission standards for CO2 is because he noted CO2 was not considered a pollutant under the Clean Air Act and that regulating CO2 will lead to higher energy prices by changing from coal to natural gas. What an excuse!!

President Bush Continues To Attack The Environment To The Delight of Lumber, Oil and Mining Interests

I suppose Dubya thinks that with a very high approval rating (high 80s) he can get away with whatever he wants. And he is trying to do just that with assaults on civil liberties and now a return to attack/assault the environment. Does he realize that his 80-something percent approval rating is not for his domestic efforts or policies. It is purely a response to the terrorist attack on America and the loss of about 5,000 lives. I hope he does not read too much into his current approval rating.

So what has Dubya done to the environment this time? The New York Times (Nov. 18, 2001) reported that "In the last two months, the Bush administration has proceeded with several regulations, legal settlements and legislative measures intended to reverse Clinton-era environmental policies.

While the nation is concentrating on Osama bin Laden, Afghanistan and anthrax, Dubya is quietly mounting other assaults on the homefront hoping no one pays attention and hoping that his deceptive high approval rating will carry him through.

Election

Florida Election Controversy Continues

The U.S. Commission on Civil Rights released preliminary report yesterday that blamed Florida officials especially Governor Jeb Bush and Sec. of State Katherine Harris for being "grossly derelict" and showing "lack of leadership" which 'led to the disenfranchisement of countless Floridians, a majority of whom were African-Americans" according to the Washington Post (June 5, 2001) and other publications. The W/Post indicated that Jeb Bush and Ms. Harris "'choose to simply ignore the mounting evidence' that voters were having serious problems on Election Day, perpetuating 'a pattern and practice of injustice, ineptitude and inefficiency' that denied them the right to vote'."

The Commission is composed of four Democrats, three independents and one Republicans. Two members of the Commission (Abigail Thernstrom, Republican and Russell Redenbaugh, Independent) have denounced the draft report as biased. So the controversy continues. Those who do not like the conclusions have condemned it. That has caused the Chairwoman, Mary Frances Berry, to dismiss the charges by the opposition.

According to the New York Times (June 6, 2001), Gov. Jeb Bush through his general counsel has "…dismissed the findings as irresponsible and biased." If the findings were the other way round, Gov. Bush and the rest of the Bush supporters will hail it. Now that it is not in their favor, they dismiss the contents. Never mind all the open hearings and efforts of the Commission and all the hard work they put into it.

Immigration

In Agreement With Dubya....On Immigration

I promised to praise Dubya when he does or says something I like. The real test is implementation. Dubya has indicated he would like the Immigration section of the Justice Department to hasten the time it takes to process immigration papers and in granting citizenships to immigrants. I'm in total agreement with him on that and I hope he backs up his rhetoric with funds and necessary number of personnel to get the job done.

I hope he does not disappoint me on that pledge. He made similar pledge during the campaign. Immigrants have contributed tremendously to the development (economic, technological, politically, socially, etc) of the USA. No doubt in my mind that America would not be what it is today without the positive contributions of immigrants. There are lots of bottlenecks and frustration associated with processing immigration papers and bringing relatives from overseas. It would be great if the time it takes is cut down drastically.

Permanent Residency For Illegal Mexicans?

Where are the voices of those Bush supporters and right-wingers who would have screamed to high heavens if the Clinton/Gore administration considered granting legal status to more than 3 million illegal Mexican nationals residing in the U.S.? I do not hear them as President Bush considers to do just that.

I point this out not because I am against the move but to emphasize the hypocrisy and double standard involved. Many Republicans/right-wingers actually thought and probably still think that Clinton won reelection in 1996 because he granted citizenships to "illegal foreign nationals" especially Mexicans. Of course that was not the reason Clinton won again. In my view, he won because he had better ideas and policies than Dole and the Republicans.

So why is Dubya considering this? I think it is all political. He probably thinks they will all vote for him in the next election. I also think he is being influenced by Mexican president Vicente Fox who favors such a policy. It is all about that 'personal relationship' Dubya has developed with the man. Apparently Mr. Fox is Dubya's closest foreign ally. He knew him while he was the Texas governor.

I have got some news for Dubya. If he thinks additional 3 million former illegal Mexicans will help him win reelection, he is mistaken. All and probably most of them will not vote for him once they discover the type of policies he favors besides immigration. I think Dubya is hoping that the 3 million or more Mexican nationals will become a voting block like Cuban-Americans who vote mostly for the Republicans. The two populations are different and are in the U.S. under different circumstances --political for Cuban-Americans and economic for Mexican-Americans.

I have indicated in the past that I support Dubya's attempt to encourage the INS to speed up immigration process for legal citizens filing for their relatives who reside overseas. If he considers granting legal status for illegal Mexican-Americans, I hope he does so for illegal

Africans, Asians, Europeans and others from around the world including Latin-Americans. It is only fair. They are already here in the U.S.

Is This The Rational To Legalize More Than 3 Milliom Illegal Mexicans?

I think I discovered the rational behind President Bush administration's plan to legalize more than 3 million illegal Mexicans in the U.S.A. By the way I'm aware there is talk of lowering that number to less than 3 million following criticisms of the plan by sources including some conservatives. One thing is clear. Dubya and his administration want to legalize millions of Mexican immigrants.

For the record, I support the idea as long as the same is extended to other nationalities and illegal immigrants including other Latin American nationals, Africans, Asians, Europeans and others. Fair is fair.

I concluded Dubya is considering legalizing illegal Mexicans for political reasons. He wants their vote and he hopes such votes and other Hispanic votes will win the reelection for him in 2004. I think most people understand that.

From all I read from various press reports, the rationale for the proposed legalization became obvious to me. It was Karl Rove's idea. He already calculated that Bush would win reelection in 2004 if the Republicans can get about 3 million more votes than they received in 2000. He thought he could get those votes by legalizing more than three million illegal Mexicans.

The only question that kept wandering in my mind is "How or what makes Karl Rove think three million newly legalized Mexican immigrants will vote Republican?" There is no guarantee about that because a lot of them could end up voting for the Democrats as the majority of Hispanics and Latinos do.

Jokes, Gaffes and 'Bushism's'

"Bushisms" (A Dozen Samples; Courtesy of Jacob Weisberg, Slate Magazine.)

1. "As governor of Texas, I have set high standards for our public schools, and I have met those standards."—CNN online chat, Aug. 30, 2000

2. "Well, I think that if you say you're going to do something and don't do it, that's trustworthiness."—ibid

3. "We cannot let rouge terrorists and rouge nations hold this nation hostile or hold our allies hostile."—Ibid

4. "I have a different vision of leadership. A leadership is someone who brings people together." Aug. 18, 2000

5. "This case has had full analyzation and has been looked at a lot. I understand the emotionality of death penalty cases." June 23, 2000.

6. "The only things I can tell you is that every case I have reviewed I have been comfortable with the innocence or guilt of the person that I've looked at. I do not believe we've put a guilty—I mean innocent personto death in the state of Texas." June 16, 2000

7. "I hope we get to the bottom of the answer. It's what I'm interested to know."—On what happened in negotiations between the Justice Department and Elian Gonzalez's Miami relatives, as quoted by the Associated Press, April 26, 2000

8. "If you are sick and tired of the politics of cynicism and polls and principles, come and join this campaign." Hilton Head, S.C. Feb. 16, 2000

9. "The most important job is not to be governor, or first lady in my case." (Quoted in San Antonio Express-News, Jan. 30, 2000

10. "What I'm against is quotas. I am against hard quotas, quotas they basically delineated based upon whatever. However they delineate, quotas, I think vulcanize society. So I don't know how that fits into what everybody else is saying, their relative positions, but that's my position." Jan. 21, 2000

11. "Keep good relations with the Grecians."—Quoted in the Economist, June 12, 1999

12. "Kosovians can move back in."—CNN Inside Politics, April 9, 1999

Dubya Chokes On A Pretzel

Ok. Hold on. Don't laugh yet. It sounds like a joke but it is not a joke. My ribs have been hurting since I read and heard the news. It won't be that funny if Dubya really got hurt but he is apparently fine.

The story is that Dubya and his dogs were watching a NFL game yesterday when suddenly Dubya knocked himself out with a pretzel and fainted for some seconds. No one knows exactly how long he passed out but he was unconscious for sometime. Dubya claimed it must have been for a very short time because when he woke up, the dogs were still in the same position they were when he fainted. Really?

His spokesman, Ari Fleischer later indicated the dogs were looking at him funny when he woke up. This is just too funny. I suspect even some of Dubya supporters will get a belly laugh out of this. Just think we did not have a conscious president for sometime and Cheney was no where around and did not know what happened. Now go ahead and laugh if you want because even the president made a lot of fun about himself because of the incident. He reminded the nation and the world that he did not listen to his mother's advise because mother told him to always chew his pretzel before he swallowed it. The president also gave away bags of pretzels to reporters who traveled with him right after the incident. The reporters were at the back of Air Force One.

For How Long Will the "Liberal Press" Ignore Gov. Bush's Lies and Shameful Gaffes?

This is one of the articles I wrote during the presidential campaign of 2000. Ok, I have heard enough about Gore and his "lies" and "misrepresentations" from right-wingers and the "liberal press." The fact is that most of the "lies" attributed to Gore are not lies. Right-wingers in most cases twisted what the man said and gave it a whole new meaning. I will rather have Gore defend himself but I'm really getting tired of reading or hearing right-wingers misrepresent the facts.

Mr. Gore himself has to be very careful about what he says because right-wingers are watching every word for the interest of giving what he says a different meaning. Mr. Gore has even be forced to apologize and he has promised to be more careful about his statements. It is good he made an apology but for what? He is apologizing and promising to check out his facts properly while Dubya keeps committing unlimited number of gaffes and telling lies that for the most part is under reported or never reported or emphasized. He utters nonsense repeatedly and even he cannot figure out what he said or meant. Where is the fairness in reporting? Right-wingers are running away with their concocted lies about Gore and it appears Democrats are finally waking up to refute such concocted lies.

Did Gore receive a letter from a parent in Florida about an overcrowded classroom? Yes he did. Did he make up that story? No he did not. Where is the lie? Did the parents of the student back up the letter they wrote to Gore? Yes, they did. To me Gore should not be apologizing about this. He did not forge the letter. If he did, I will be among the first to condemn him.

Gore was right in emphasizing that the top one percent in income receives most of the benefits in Dubya's tax cut plans. He is right and Dubya could not and cannot refute that. All Dubya could do is accuse him of "fuzzy math" but he knows Gore is right. He did not lie. Dubya is the one that lies by not telling the tax payers how exactly the benefits of his tax cuts will be distributed. Then again, he has had problems explaining it or understanding it himself. The Republican Congressional candidates are running away from Dubya's tax cut plans and priorities in this election. That's how much confidence they have in it.

Was Gore right in telling Dubya in their first debate that he (Dubya) should not be inviting the Russians to help resolve the uprising in Yugoslavia? Yes, Gore was right because at the time, Russia still supported Milosevic and did not recognize the new leadership. I see nothing wrong with what Gore said. He was right but somehow, right-wingers including Dubya supporters found a way to contradict his thoughts with the president's policy. It makes you wonder when they became such good friends of President Clinton.

Did Gore visit disaster-inflicted areas in Texas? Yes, he did but not at the same time with Mr. Witt for that that particular disaster. Leaving the impression that he accompanied Mr. Witt on that particular visit is misleading. He has accompanied him on several other vists to disaster areas including Texas. So he went to the disaster area and that to me is the main point about that. Gore has apologized for the misrepresentation and "embellishment" also. Meanwhile, Dubya has not and does not apologize for his lies, embellishments and shameful gaffes. Where is the fairness in reporting?

Democrats for the most part have been rather dormant while right-wingers pile on Gore. They have been more into running a positive campaign while Dubya and his camp dish out one negative comment and advertisement after another. Apparently, it seems that it finally dawned on Democrats to wake up before right-wingers suffocate them with their concocted lies and misrepresentations.

Finally, Democrats (in higher places in the campaign) have decided to point out not only Dubya's lies, but his "confused, bumbling, babbling and ignorant" self. It's about time. I do not think there is anything negative about those as long as the facts and references are accurate. I think it is important to point those out. They would be in any other local, state or national election. Those are nothing compared to the presidential elections. Why shouldn't they be pointed out? If the

Democratic candidate gaffed and spaced out like Dubya when he is asked questions, this contest would have been over a long time ago in favor of the Republican candidate.

I have written about Dubya's gaffes, verbal and factual blunders in the past. It took sometime but I see many more Democrats and some in the "liberal press" are now closely examining Dubya's gaffes, embellishments, lies and misrepresentations.

Last week in Wisconsin, Dubya reminded many viewers on TV why his reputation is that of the bumbling and confused candidate. A woman asked him what she would tell a friend to make her vote for him. Ladies and gentlemen, what and who I saw was Dubya at his worst. I thought I had seen him at his worst before that moment but he surpassed himself. That was horrible. Maybe you saw the same picture. It was shown briefly on Meet the Press with Tim Russert. For more than three minutes, Dubya did not have an answer for the woman. It was pathetic as he searched for the right answers. I could not believe it. Apparently he does not know why he is running for the presidency. Shameful!! According to ABCNEWS, Dubya finally said, "Tell her to keep an open mind…No. Tell her governments don't create wealth…You know that…Here's what I'd tell her…Fellow's got a pretty good record and he's done in office what he said he would…" Finally, after searching for answers, Dubya admitted, "I'm groping for the right answer, you can tell-weaving around." That was unbelieveable!!!

The second presidential debate is tonight. The "liberal press" and right-wingers can spend all their time ignoring the issues while talking about Gore's "heavy breathing" and "sighs" from the first debate. I heard Dubya on the radio yesterday talk about the election being "4 days away" rather than 4 weeks away." He did correct himself. The "liberal press" can waste all their time talking negatively about Gore while Dubya continues to demonstrate that he is confused by the complexity of the office he seeks and that he lacks the knowledge and experience required for the position he seeks. Gore is and was right about that. I don't even know why he was trying to mellow his thoughts about that. Dubya does not have the experience or at least enough of the experience required for the office of the president.

One more example of Dubya's lies. How many times have you heard Dubya say he does not base his decisions on polls or focus groups? He says he bases what he does in the campaign on what he thinks. Well, that is a lie because a lot of what he does in this campaign is based on polls and focus groups. Have you seen anyone question Dubya on that lie of his? The fact is that both leading campaigns use polls and focus groups.

Dubya has reinvented himself several times in this campaign (as I wrote before) based on poll numbers and focus groups. It was the reason he dropped "compassionate conservatism" message for "real plans for real people." Today, it appears to be "Blueprint for the Future" sprinkled with "Tools for Parents" which I see on some of the podiums he speaks (no, mangles) from.

MSNBC (Oct. 6, 2000) confirmed what I have always known and written about. The report indicated that "the George W. Bush team has spent nearly $850,000" on polling. Why is Dubya not scrutinized for his lies? Tell me again that the press is "liberal". If the press is so "liberal", why do they largely continue to ignore Dubya's lies, embellishments (as in his prescription drug plans), and unbelievable and worse- than-Quayle's gaffes?

Dubya's So-called Jokes: Still Funny To You?

At the 2001 correspondents dinner last week, Dubya continued with his jokes. Dubya is supposedly poking fun at himself. The weak-in-the-knees press laughed and some thought he was "Charming". Like I indicated in a previous article, "Is the Joke On You", I do not find many of Dubya's jokes about himself funny because they seem to be very close to the truth.

I think it is his way of trying to disarm the press. Guess what, the press seems to be timid when it comes to Dubya and they still do not ask him tough questions. He found a way to control them. Just examine the interviews Dubya had with different persons in the media to reflect on his first 100 days in office. In one interview for example, Dubya spoke about his commitment to the environment and his plans to resolve the energy crisis. Just smooth talking. On energy, the reporter could not even ask him simple follow up questions such as Dubya's plan to cut funding for research into technology and conservation efforts. None. Dubya just controlled the press and told them all he wanted. The press chickened out. What a joke!!

Speaking about jokes, what about that nude picture of his little brother (Jeb) that Dubya showed to the whole world? Was that a good idea? Was that really funny? If Clinton did anything like that, he would have gotten an earful from Clinton haters and other right-wingers. They would have castigated him as usual and probably accused him of promoting child pornography. The conservative right-wing hate radio would be buzzing about the same issue for sometime.

Quoting Dubya: Please Do Not Repeat In Your English Class

This quote is two days old but given the release of Americans in China, it is still very fresh. Grammatically, it is something else. I watched on television as President Bush met with King Abdallah Hussein of Jordan. When asked about the crew held in China, Dubya indicated his administration was working hard "…to bring the solution to an end." The "solution to an end"? It made no sense but that is Dubya-talk and only our president can and does get away with such an abuse of the English language.

I am certainly not perfect with my English but I expect our president to do better. I and others pointed that out during the campaign but it did not matter. I listened to King Hussein and he had a command of the English Language, for someone who English is his second or third language. He was excellent. I could not say so for my president.

President "Dubya" Bush: The Joke Is On Us--This Is Not Funny

Dubya appeared at the Gridiron Club's 116th annual spoof on Saturday night. First of all, whether it is Dubya, Clinton, Reagan, Ford, Carter and so on, I do not think it is a fantastic idea to have the press wining and dining with the president or the chief executive they are supposed to cover. In the case of Dubya, the press has helped him all along by not asking him any serious or challenging questions. He benefits even more by cozying up with the press and I do not think it is in the best interest of the governed. I can devote an article or two about this but that is not the reason I'm writing at the moment.

I write my opinions and my observations. The so-called "liberal press" are in many ways in bed with Dubya so they will not write pointed opinions as I write at times. Moreover, I'm under no one's authority with regard to anyone telling me what to write or not write. I have no one paying me salaries for writing. So I write what comes to my mind without being unnecessarily malicious about it. To me it is the truth although my right-wing opponents will argue about that but what else is new.

So let me get to the point. The March 25, 2001 a certain headline was on one of the news channels. It read, "Bush leaves Gridiron Club laughing." The same day, the nytimes.com headline read, "Bush Pokes Fun at Perception." As far as I am concerned, a better title is "The Joke is on Us--This is not Funny." I have two other perfect titles for Dubya's appearance at the Gridiron on Saturday. One is "Is it Real or is it Memorex" (borrowing from an old commercial from years ago featuring jazz great Ella Fitzgerald) and the other is "When Perception is Reality."

Dubya's jokes would be funny to me but the "jokes" he used were so close to reality. For me, it was not a matter of perception as it was a matter of reality. It was not funny because the things he put down (or someone put down for him as 'jokes" were real. I probably would not mind that much if we were speaking about any other person. In this case, we are talking about the president of the United States.

The president admitted jokingly during the dinner that he suffers from foot-in-mouth disease his lips are where words go and die. He also joked he hoped to clone another Dick Cheney so he won't have to do any work. It is good the president is poking fun at himself but on a second thought, I do not find some of his jokes funny. They seem real rather than joking matter. Is the joke on you?

Is This Supposed To Be Funny? President "Dubya" Bush Once Again Confirms He Is Syntactically-Challenged

I'm beginning to wonder what some of those who voted for Dubya must be thinking about now. Oh no, I'm not talking or writing about his fellow right-wing supporters. They are willing to quickly abandon their distaste for lies and deceits in support of the flip-flopping and lying Dubya. I'm wondering specifically about some of those "undecided" who voted for Dubya. I wonder what they are thinking now.

Just a few days ago (March 26, 2001), I wrote about "President 'Dubya" Bush: The Joke Is On Us: This Is Not Funny." Only three days later, he continued to 'joke' at the radio and TV correspondents' dinner. He once again confirms what may know about him. He told those in attendance (and the rest of the nation and the world) that he is syntax-challenged. We knew that. He joked about some of the statements he mangled in the past, some of which made no sense at all. Are we supposed to be laughing? Is this supposed to be funny? I don't think so. Not surprisingly, the "liberal press' reported Dubya "stole the show with self-depreciating wit and charm…" It is one reason I refer to the press at times as "Weak-in-the-knees". How much "wit and charm" is there for a president who has noticable problems reading or putting sentences together? This is not funny, witty or charming.

Demonstrating that the joke is on us, and his lack of environmental awareness, Dubya told the audience, "As you know, we're studying safe levels for arsenic in drinking water…To base our decision on sound science, the scientists told us we needed to test the water glasses of about 3,000 people. Thank you for participating." I really think that somehow, Dubya thinks he can joke his way through anything including dropping the requirements for arsenic in drinking water. How funny is that?

In demonstrating some of his confused and syntactically-challenged statements, he attempted a joke but it was not funny to me. For example, "I know the human being and the fish can coexist peacefully…I understand small business growth. I was one." With regard to the last statement he admitted, "I don't have the slightest idea what I was saying." Right there, Dubya spoke the truth. Not only was he unable to understand what he was talking about, many others (or should I say millions of others) including myself had no idea what he was talking about.

I probably would laugh if all were in the past. Unfortunately, Dubya is still the same person. The correspondents' dinner was on Thursday and he addressed the press the next day. His performance at such appearances (including with visiting heads of state) with regards to his answers to the questions and his syntax is less than presidential and unsatisfactory. Only his staunch supporters and right-wingers will ignore all that and attack you for pointing them out. Will they attack Dubya for pointing out some of his faults too? I don't think so.

Missile Defense

Putin Says "No" Again To Abandoning ABM Treaty

One again, President Putin of Russia has rejected any thoughts of the Bush administration unilaterally abandoning the ABM Treaty. He made it clear to the visiting U.S. Defense Secretary, Mr. Donald Rumsfeld.

It's clear to me where Putin and Russia stand on ABM treaty. They want the treaty to remain and not abandoned. Maybe the Bush administration think they can convince him (Putin) to change his mind. They are trying but it is not working. Bush has tried. It did not work. He sent Condelezza Rice. It did not work. Now he sent Mr. Rumsfeld. It is not working. What will it take for the Bush administration to understand it is barking on the wrong tree?

The Press

Dubya: "I Don't Have Anthrax.": If He Could Only Answer The Question He Was Asked

I hope you heard it or saw the president on television reacting to a question he was not asked. Sure we are in a 'war' but we still have our Dubya and like I promised many times, I keep an eye on Dubya because I have observed and documented many times that what he says are often different from what he does. He tries so much to present a 'good guy' image but on close examination, the character is something else. Examples include his flip-flops, his refusal to answer important questions, his techniques of saying or doing almost anything to defeat or get rid of his political opponents. And I'm not just writing about Gore. John McCain experienced some of Dubya's techniques including the Republican primaries when an advertisement supporting Bush questioned McCain's hero status during the 2000 South Carolina primary. This was from a man who avoided Vietnam and who reportedly was on AWOL from Air Force for an extended period. Of course he never discussed his 'wild and crazy days' or if he ever did hard drugs or even smoked marijuana. Every other presidential candidate at the time answered to whether he smoked marijuana or ingested other drugs in their youth or in their past. Mr. Bush refused to answer that question. Talk about character. Then we found out very late in the presidential campaign in 2000 about his Driviing Under the Influence of alcohol (DUI) record which he never brought up because 'he did not want his children to know." Really? How about some rather truthful answers like it could hurt his chances of running for Congress, governor or the presidency?

Back to my main topic. Dubya was asked a simple question. He gave an answer that was not asked. A Dubya-like answer that only raised more questions or made one curious. That was my reaction. So what was the question? Quote, "Mr. President, have you or the Vice President been tested for anthrax?" Dubya answered, "First of all, I don't have anthrax." The reporter asked again, "Mr President, have you been tested for anthrax?" In which Dubya responded again, "I don't have anthrax." The reporter asked again, "So you've been tested, sir?" One more time, Dubya responded, "I don't have it."

I do not know how others reacted to Dubya's answers but it made me shake my head. Answering questions or a question that was not asked only raises the level of curiousity and invites more questions. Could it be that Dubya has isolated himself so much from reporters that even the simplest of questions are too complicated for him to answer? He should talk to reporters more and have more press conferences so he can be more comfortable talking. I observed during the 2000 presidential campaign that he approached every reporter's question with suspicion. Is like "they are not going to get me." He does not have to think that every question is a trap to get him or to trick him. Unfortunately, he thinks that way and I believe that is why he hardly meets the press.

Looking Back and Forward: The "Liberal Press" Has Been Very Very Good To Bush

I pulled out a Washington Post article by Howard Kurtz dated July 27, 2000. This was in the summer of 2001. It was entitled "Pew Poll: Voters Reject Media Message". I was looking for another evidence (as if I needed more) to back up my assertion that the press have been licking Dubya's boots for a long time. Many of us know that but I know there are those who do not believe my assertion due to partisan political blindness. I also wanted to figure out why Dubya keeps getting away with a lot of lies and still most of the so called 'liberal press' do not call it like it is.

According to the W/Post article from about a year ago, George W. Bush has enjoyed considerable success selling himself as a different kind of politician, with more than half his media coverage this year revolving around that theme. Yet a slightly higher percentage of the public associates that description with Vice President Gore."

Back to the article. Quote, "Equally important, the study found, a stunning 76% of the coverage of Gore focused on two negative themes-that he lies and exaggerates, and is tarred by scandal. This contrasted dramatically with the most common theme about Bush, that he is a different kind of Republican..." 'A different kind of Republican'? We shall see.

Dubya: The Press Is Licking His Boots: I Knew I'm Not The Only One Who Has Noticed

I have written about the lazy press. I have written about the "weak-in-the-knees" (my words) press. I have discounted and disagreed with those who insist the press is "liberal". I have commented often about the inability of the press to ask Dubya relevant and challenging questions. I have compared the way the press treated President Clinton to how they treated candidate Bush and how they are treating President Bush so far. I have written all that and more.

Some in the opposition attribute my kind of observations about Bush as whining. I just wish at least someone in the opposition can respond truthfully to the observation that Dubya has essentially has a free ride with the press.

I see in the Washington Post (May 14, 2001) that there are others who feel the same way I do and who observe the same things I have observed. It is good to see because it shows I'm not alone on this. There are people who are very upset about the issue. According to the article by Howard Kurtz in the Washington Post, "Some of those who wrote letters (to him) are hardly neutral, referring to Bush as an "idiot"," "illegitimate," "arrogant," "Shrub," "Resident Bush" or "Dumbya." Many question why incidents from Bush's past—such as his driving-under-the-influence conviction or alleged absence from the National Guard—have not received tougher scrutiny."

The article continued; "Most say the press was terribly unfair to Clinton—and argue, for example, that there would have been far more coverage if Chelsea Clinton, not Jenna Bush, had been arrested for possession of alcohol. Most complain about inadequate examination of Bush's policies on energy and the environment or his Texas record—which have been widely reported, despite the upbeat tone of much of the Bush coverage. I have written about Dubya's record in Texas? I wrote specifically about his environmental records, his housing record and his educational record.

What I found very interesting in the Kurtz's article is the individual reactions. For example, Karen Sandness (Portland, Oregon) wrote, "I was always a lukewarm supporter of Bill Clinton…but I'm so upset with the media coverage of George W. Bush…that I no longer watch television news or give much credence to what I read in the main stream press.

My favorite of those who wrote is Laurel Wiegert of Denver. She is my favorite because she expressed her view and made it known she is not a Democrat. She wrote: "The media at large is completely licking Bush's boots. It's sad—and disgusting. In case it matters, I am NOT a Democrat!" There were other comments in similar tone but anyone can go to my source and read the rest of them if the person chooses to do so.

In closing, I will end this article with one specific example as we await Dubya's energy policy this week. I think we already know the bulk of it. I think it is "explore, explore, explore and drill, drill, and drill." It is also "coal and nuclear power plant for every city." Never mind their environmental drawbacks. I know I'm exaggerating about the policy but it is not too far from their intentions if they had their way. Part of the energy policy in my opinion will pay lip service to "conservation" after all the criticisms Dubya and Cheney received for initially dismissing conservation (especially Cheney).

I also expect part of the policy to pay lip service to "new technologies." I say so about new technologies because while Dubya talks about it, he cut funding in his budget that will be used towards developing those new technologies. I'm yet to hear a member of the press question Dubya why he did that or why he says one thing and does the other. Dubya has effectively kept the press away from him. Press conference notices are given shortly before Dubya appears at the podium. The press just sits there laughing nervously (as they laughed in all those reporters' dinner events about Dubya's jokes). Well, the joke is on them.

Illustrating Right-Wing Lunacy

An Illustration Of Right Wing and Gun-Loving Lunacy

In one of my classes at the university, I had a student who illustrated the lunacy of right- wing, gun-loving frame of mind and thought process. He indicated in the class that he has been described as "right-wing." I have been teaching for eight years at the time and I very rarely discuss or write about my students. I decided to write about this particular student (the name is obviously not important) because two of his statements in two weeks affirmed one of the primary reasons I love to teach. Students normally take classes to obtain credits towards graduation. I always tell my students that credits are very important but the lifetime knowledge that is or that can be obtained while seeking those credits are even more important.

I had a gentleman in my class who was calm outwardly. He appeared to be his late thirties or early forties. He was a good student and scored excellent grades. He attended classes regularly. He also had a family with a wife and children.

He contributed to discussions in the class. Within two weeks, he made two different statements that gave me the opportunity to challenge him further. His statements were in relation to our discussion in class. When the topic of the United Nations came up he indicated he does not like the United Nations because they were going to take guns away from Americans. I was very surprised and stunned by his statement. I asked him how or where he learnt that. He said that's what he heard. I told him it is not true because the UN do not have such a mission. Without going into details, it is pertinent to indicate how his statement came about. As the teacher, I discussed the formation of the

117

UN, the number of countries in the UN, the various organizations within the UN such as the Food and Agriculture Organization (FAO), the World Health Organization (WHO), and the United Nations Educational, Scientific and Cultural Organization (UNESCO). I further discussed the role of the UN and its strengths and weaknesses. Based on the discussion in the class, I inquired if they knew why the U.S. has refused to pay its dues to the UN. It was at that point that the student made his statement.

The following week, while discussing America's National Park Service (NPS), I indicated it is the most copied American institution. Some might think it is democracy, freedom or system of government. Not at all. The NPS is the most copied because more that 125 countries have adopted the system. In discussing the topic, I indicated the beginning, the extent and the management of the federally-owned parks. At that point, my otherwise calm and good student interrupted, "I thought the park system is owned by the UN." He stunned me again but as always, I maintained my composure. I asked him how he learnt that. He told me he heard it from "someone at work." I suggested some readings for him. He promised do so before talking to the person that told him the UN owns the NPS. I asked him to talk to that person because the information s/he gave is wrong.

What did I learn from my anti-UN student? I learnt a lot. To actually hear and talk to someone who believed what he believed about the UN was very revealing to me. I see how much some (especially right-wing) anti-UN rhetoric and misinformation has spread across America. You hear it a lot on right-wing talk shows but I never thought I would meet someone who actually believed that kind of misinformation. Moreover, my student is an adult and a family man. I wondered (to myself) whether he teaches or feeds his children that kind of wrong information. Another reason I was stunned and remain stunned is that the student already had a degree and is working on his Masters degree. Unfortunately, he is not the only one that thinks like that. There are a lot of people with and without much education who believe like he does. I'm a lot more disturbed or concerned when supposedly well-educated people with college degrees think that way. I wonder whether those kinds of individuals are just too lazy to read or properly research the information for themselves. How could anyone walk around with such thoughts—thoughts they heard from someone else who heard it from someone else and so on. I'm glad I'm teaching because it gives me an opportunity to correct some of those lunatic and ridiculous thoughts and beliefs.

Isolation

How Isolationist Can Dubya Get?

R ight about now with only seven months I hope it is clear why some feared the possibility of Dubya residing in the White House. Some feared so much they indicated they would leave the country if he won. Not a good idea if you ask me. I would rather stay and watch his plans and policies and document them—so that three to four years from now during re-election, he and his supporters will not have to tell me about his "wonderful character honor and reign". I guess strongly that even some of his supporters will not be fooled again.

I will not blame whoever is leaving the country but I would wish they stay back and fight against his hurtful policies. Dubya is not only busy guiding the US domestically in the wrong direction with his policies such as energy, environment, tax cuts, social security, Patients Bill of Rights, etc, he wants to isolate the US from the rest of the world in several areas.

How about this record of isolationism? There is the Kyoto/Bonn accord, global warming problem, ABM Treaty, missile defense, germ warfare and the latest is the threat to pull the US out of the conference on racism in Durban, South Africa. Can Dubya and those who voted for him take responsibility for the way the US is losing its leadership role in the world because of Dubya reckless leadership?

What's The Hoopla About What Sen. Daschle Said?

What is the hoopla about what Sen. Tom Daschle said about President Bush? This is one of those "Much Ado About Nothing" that characterize a lot of Republican criticisms in my opinion. Why is the so-called "liberal press" and certainly the conservative press led by talking heads on the hate radio trying to convince the rest of us that Mr. Daschle committed an abominable offense by criticizing the president while he is overseas just because Mr. Daschle indicated that Dubya is being an "isolationist" with his foreign policy. What's wrong with that? Why is Mr. Daschle being persecuted because he said the truth?

I just have a few quick comments about the hoopla because I got tired of hearing about it. First, the president was on his way overseas when Mr. Daschle made his statement in an interview. Frankly, it does not matter to me whether the president was on his way or on the ground in another country. The truth is the truth.

Second, Mr. Daschle should not have apologized or regretted the timing of the statement.

He solidly "stands by" his statement as he should but I do not think he has anything to regret or apologize for. Third, I do not think his (Daschle's) freedom of speech should be limited because the president is flying overseas or in another nation. Fourth, and this is for those with very short memories; former House Speaker Newt Gingrich and his Whip Tom Delay said even worse and harsher things about President Clinton while he was overseas at different times. Other Republicans including talking heads on hate radio made even more cruel statements.

Tom Daschle is right. President Bush is pursuing an 'isolationist' policy with regard to his stance on Kyoto accord, global warming, missile defense and ABM Treaty. What's wrong with what Mr. Daschle said? Nothing in my opinion and you should have known that if you have been reading my articles on this site.

The View from Overseas

Dubya's Image and Leadership: European Poll That Agrees With Me (And Millions of Others)

I have written in the past that Dubya's image and leadership have unfavorable ratings in Europe and around the world. I have described his image as "poor at best" in many European countries. His "my way or no way" approach on treaties is frowned upon by most people and countries around the world. They see that as arrogance. His inability to articulate and explain his views does not help either.

According to a New York Times report by Adam Clymer (remember him? The one Dubya cussed out during the campaign), "Ordinary Europeans strongly back their political leaders unhappiness with American foreign policy on specific issues like the Kyoto environmental treaty and the Bush administration's threat to withdraw from the 1972 Antiballistic Missile Treaty, polls in France, Germany, Great Britain and Italy show."

The normal response of right-wingers or Dubya supporters to polls like this involving Europe comes in various variations like "Who cares"? They are Europeans, who cares about what they say or think? This is America and the president represents America, not Europe and so on."

I have news for right-wingers, Dubya supporters and those in Dubya administration who dismisses what Europeans think or say. You better listen and pay attention. How is Dubya going to work with the European allies if most of the European leaders and the people disagree with his policies? How much does Dubya want to carry on with his isolationist policies? Can he really dismiss the rest of the world or most of it with "I don't care" attitude? I do not think he and America can afford to do so.

Dubya is not only hurting his image at home and abroad with his policies, he is hurting America and it is incumbent on Americans to speak up and act before he does further damage.

0-595-22114-9

www.ingramcontent.com/pod-product-compliance
Lightning Source LLC
Chambersburg PA
CBHW020249290526
45784CB00003B/1166